THE NAKED QUAKER

DIANE RAPAPORT

The Naked Quaker

True Crimes and Controversies from the
Courts of Colonial New England

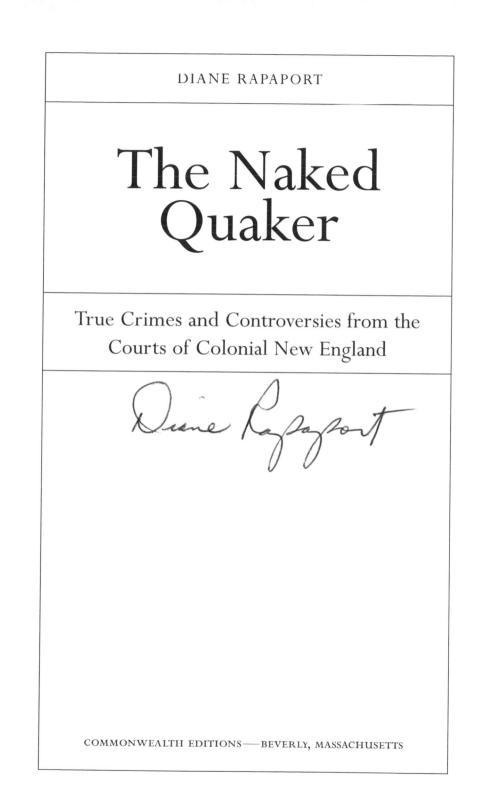

COMMONWEALTH EDITIONS—BEVERLY, MASSACHUSETTS

ISBN: 978-1-933212-96-8

Originally published in hardcover
(ISBN: 978-1-933212-57-9)

Library of Congress Cataloging-in-Publication Data
Rapaport, Diane.
  The Naked Quaker : true crimes and controversies from the courts of colonial New England / Diane Rapaport.
     p. cm.
  Includes bibliographical references and index.
  ISBN 978-1-933212-96-8 (alk. paper)
  1. Crime--New England--History--17th century. 2. Trials--New England--History--17th century. 3. Dispute resolution (Law)--New England--History--17th century. 4. Court records--New England--History--17th century. 5. New England--History--17th century. I. Title.
  HV6793.N295R36 2007
  364.10974'09032--dc22
                                        2007025267

Cover design by John Barnett.

Printed in the United States of America.

Commonwealth Editions is an imprint of Memoirs Unlimited, Inc., 266 Cabot Street, Beverly, Massachusetts 01915. Visit us on the Web at www.commonwealtheditions.com

10 9 8 7 6 5 4 3 2

CONTENTS

To my Quaker great-grandmother,
Anna Laura Webster Day,
1863–1928

She never appeared naked in public (so far as I know!),
but she defied her own religious community in a
different way and followed her heart.
I hope, one day, to tell her story.

PREFACE

I LOVE READING old court records, which can be stranger than fiction and just as entertaining. No other source offers such intimate and surprising detail about the past, bringing history—and our ancestors—to life. I especially enjoy court cases from Puritan New England, which I share in this book and in my award-winning "Tales from the Courthouse" column for *New England Ancestors* magazine, where many of the true stories in *The Naked Quaker* first appeared.

Readers often ask me how I found these stories, and I never have a short answer, for my path to this book was decades in the making. Although I studied colonial America in college and earned a B.A. degree in history, I never looked at court records until I went on to law school and became a trial lawyer. Even then, while practicing law in Minneapolis and later in Boston, the only court records I read were relatively modern ones. I never imagined becoming a historical author or writing a book called *The Naked Quaker*. But life takes unexpected twists and turns, and chance encounters can alter careers. I still remember the moment about ten years ago that launched me in a new professional direction, when I happened to open a book about the history of my town, Lexington, Massachusetts.

As I turned the pages, one paragraph caught my eye, about a Scottish soldier, William Munro, who arrived in Lexington (then called Cambridge Farms) during the mid-1600s. Captured by Oliver Cromwell's troops during the English Civil War, Munro and hundreds of other Scottish prisoners were exiled across the ocean, sold to English colonists, and forced to labor at towns and farms all over New England. They did not face a lifetime of servitude—their terms averaged five to eight years—but they were unwilling immigrants, and I had never heard their story before.

Intrigued, I wanted to learn more about Munro and his fellow Scots. I soon discovered, however, that few history or genealogy books mentioned the seventeenth-century Scottish prisoners; their story seemed to be a forgotten chapter of our New England heritage. As a lawyer, I wondered whether old court records (if they still existed) might offer more detail about what happened to these Scots as they made new lives in America. I decided to check the Massachusetts Archives, a repository of original colonial manuscripts, but I did not really expect to find anything "new." I assumed that previous generations of researchers already had mined this obvious source of historical information.

To my delight, I uncovered a wonderful cache of court files about Munro at the Massachusetts Archives, material apparently overlooked for hundreds of years, some of it in his own words. Munro's case, which I call "The Purloined Pigs," would not have garnered much publicity in its day, had newspapers existed to report on it. But Munro's lawsuit was hard-fought and emotional, and the jumble of faded handwritten documents speaks volumes about the character of this stubborn Scotsman and his neighborhood adversary. I am pleased to bring "The Purloined Pigs" out of the archives and into this book, in chapter 6. Munro also appears in another true story, "The Rhode Island Runaway," in chapter 2, which I found during that same fateful trip to the Massachusetts Archives.

Reading colonial court records became a passion (some might call it an obsession!), and I continued scouring seventeenth-century case files—at archives and in books, microfilm, and computer resources—searching for clues about the Scottish war prisoners. I found a treasure trove of information about those men and other forgotten New England ancestors (English colonists, Native Americans, African slaves, and many more)—tales too good to stay hidden away in archives—so I began writing these true stories for *New England Ancestors* and other publications. Finally, I left my law practice for full-time historical research and writing. My award-winning first book, *New England Court Records: A Research Guide for Genealogists and Historians* (Quill Pen Press, 2006), shared what I have learned about finding and using court records (not only from colonial days, but up to modern times as well). Telling stories from court cases, however, is still what I enjoy most, and *The Naked Quaker: True Crimes and Controversies from the Courts of Colonial New England* collects some of my favorites.

So many people have helped me along the way, in my transformation from trial lawyer to historical storyteller, that I can never thank them all. The folks at my publisher, Commonwealth Editions, were enthusiastic about *The Naked Quaker* from the start, and working with them on this project has been a joy. Many thanks, especially to Webster Bull, Perry McIntosh, and Diana McCloy. I also appreciate the New England Historic Genealogical Society in Boston—particularly Brenton Simons, Lynn Betlock, and Jean Powers—and the many readers of *New England Ancestors* magazine, whose encouragement and feedback played a major role in turning my "Tales from the Courthouse" column into a book. Some of the other people and organizations who offered generous assistance—contributing research help, access to records, and permission to reproduce images—are named in the Notes and Illustration Sources at the back of this book. Extra-special thanks go to my talented artist daughter, Cary Rapaport, who took time in the midst of her busy senior year at high school to create an original pen-and-ink drawing for chapter 4. Perhaps one day, after she graduates from the School of the Museum of Fine Arts in Boston (where she begins study this fall), she will illustrate future books for me!

I am also profoundly grateful, of course, to the many colonial clerks and judges who had the foresight to keep such careful court records, which now offer us a glimpse into our ancestors' past. Most of all, I wish that I could thank the long-ago New Englanders I came to know through the pages of court files. I feel privileged to tell their stories.

INTRODUCTION

FEW MODERN-DAY Americans spend much time in court. Despite the "litigation explosion" that supposedly plagues our society, most of us never enter a courthouse, and our trial experience may be limited to *Court TV.* In colonial New England, however, courts and judges played a central role in everyday life, and the old court records reveal that our ancestors were far more unruly and irreverent—and litigious—than most history books suggest. "Going to law" was the common remedy for disputes large and small—from the complicated business transactions of Atlantic shippers to neighborhood squabbles about insulting remarks or wandering livestock. And colonial judges tried to enforce strict moral standards, punishing conduct that would never be prosecuted today.

Court day was a major event in seventeenth-century New England: the local tavern was turned into a temporary courthouse, and a community's population doubled overnight as people arrived from distant towns and frontier outposts. Wealthy gentlemen mingled with petitioners and witnesses of modest means—farmers, sailors, blacksmiths, goodwives, servants, Indians—and jurors took their seats on benches in the tavern's best parlor. Judges in rich clothing (beaver-skin hats with plumes, gold-lace collars, perhaps a scarlet cloak) peered down from a long table on a specially prepared platform, as the clerk dipped his quill pen into the ink pot and called out cases from a docket.

Luckily for us, many of those colonial case files survive—on ink-splotched scraps of brittle paper in archives, on reels of microfilm, and in published volumes, CD-ROMs and online archival Web sites. Long-ago colonial New England comes to life through the pages of court records, where we experience the passions and concerns of ordinary people, sometimes in their own words, more than three hundred years after the emotion-charged events that brought them to court.

This book highlights twenty-five true colonial courtroom tales—amusing, poignant, shocking—of remarkable men and women nearly lost to history. Although our own modern world differs in profound ways from Puritan New England, these feisty characters prove that human nature changes little, no matter how many centuries pass.

THE NAKED QUAKER

Chapter 1

WITCHES
AND WILD WOMEN

The famous Salem trials of 1692 were not the first witchcraft cases in colonial New England. Other alleged witches suffered trial—and some were executed—during the earliest Puritan days. Outspoken unmarried women faced the most community suspicion and disapproval, even if they were not accused of witchcraft. The old court records reveal tantalizing details about women who simply did not fit the norms of the day, and three of those true stories take us back to the world of seventeenth-century New England.

First, "The Witch at the Top of the Stairs" tells what happened to the eccentric, middle-aged Elizabeth Godman when her New Haven neighbors began to suspect that she—and the Devil—caused strange things to happen around town. In the second story, "Watching Widow Holman," one troubled family in Cambridge, Massachusetts, pays close attention to a widow and her spinster daughter across the road. And in "A Woman of 'Enthusiastical Power,'" we meet a wild, sexy, mysterious woman of seventeenth-century New England who wields considerable influence over men.

THE WITCH AT THE TOP OF THE STAIRS

In Puritan New England virtually everyone believed in witchcraft. Ministers warned their congregations to be watchful, for the Devil recruited ordinary people as witches, and no community was safe from their evil deeds. When bad things happened—sudden deaths, strange illnesses, or crop failures— witchcraft seemed the likely explanation. Neighbors, friends, and family members might end up in court, on trial for their lives.

The most notorious New England witch trials occurred at Salem, Massa- chusetts, in 1692, but other towns throughout the region experienced witchcraft scares. Forty years before the Salem crisis, a suspected witch named Mrs. Elizabeth Godman went on trial in New Haven, Connecticut. The old court records about that case paint a revealing portrait of life in the superstitious 1600s.

Mrs. Godman lived with Deputy Governor Stephen Goodyear and his family in a large house overlooking the central town green. Perhaps she was a friend or relative of his, and she was undoubtedly a woman of high social rank, judging from her own substantial estate and the "Mrs." before her name. (In the seventeenth century "Mrs." was reserved for wives or widows of ministers and wealthy gentlemen, and sometimes for unmarried women of property.) Single women and widows, however, no matter how prosperous, could not live alone in seventeenth-century New England—the law required "family governance"—so Mrs. Godman put her financial holdings into Stephen Goodyear's hands, and he granted her a room at the top of the stairs.

From all accounts, Mrs. Godman was outspoken and opinionated, and relations with the Goodyears grew strained. With few friends and little work to occupy her time, Mrs. Godman took to wandering the New Haven streets, asking neighbors for beer and offending people with tactless or peculiar remarks. Misfortune seemed to follow visits by the eccentric Mrs. Godman: chickens dropped dead, people fell ill, and "dreadful noises" disturbed the night.

Amid a crescendo of fearful rumors, New Haven's minister preached a sermon about witches. He made no specific accusations, but he pointed out that the Devil preyed on people of a "discontented frame of spirit." Goodwife Larremore, listening in the congregation, thought immediately of Mrs. Godman and reported her suspicions to the minister.

Sooner or later, the authorities were bound to take action. Instead of waiting for the inevitable court summons, Mrs. Godman decided to file her own preemptive complaint. She sued several New Haven residents for defamation—even Deputy Governor Goodyear and his wife—and declared that she would "trounce them" all. Governor Theophilus Eaton convened a series of hearings in 1653, probably at his mansion house near the Goodyears', to learn whether the townspeople "suspected [Mrs. Godman] for a witch."

Most witnesses testified about petty matters, such as Mrs. Godman's uncanny knowledge of her neighbors' affairs. How, for example, could Mrs.

Governor Theophilus Eaton's house in New Haven Colony.

Godman know that Mrs. Atwater carried figs in her pocket or that she ate peas porridge for dinner? Mrs. Godman said that she smelled the figs and saw porridge dishes in Mrs. Atwater's kitchen, but Mrs. Atwater suspected a more sinister explanation. Other people, such as New Haven's minister, Mr. Hooke, and his Indian servant Time, reported that Mrs. Godman always "knew" what happened at church meetings, even when she did not attend. Surely the Devil (not a member of the church congregation) gave Mrs. Godman that information.

Mr. Hooke became even more suspicious when he had a dream about witches, and his son fell ill "in a very strange manner." Mrs. Godman often visited his house to "look on" the boy; did she cause the illness? The minister also revealed how Mrs. Godman confessed to troubled and disappointed feelings when New Haven's Mr. Bishop married another woman. Mrs. Godman admitted "some affection" for Mr. Bishop; was it only a coincidence that the new Mrs. Bishop suffered "very strange fits" after the wedding, and later that all of her babies died?

Many people offered similar circumstantial evidence against Mrs. Godman, but it was testimony by Stephen Goodyear's wife and adolescent daughters that proved most damning. The girls slept in a second-floor bedroom just below Mrs. Godman's chamber, and they maintained intense curiosity about their boarder's activities. Often they heard Mrs. Godman talking in her room, and on one such occasion they ran downstairs to tell their mother. Mrs. Goodyear tiptoed back up the stairs to listen outside Mrs. Godman's door, and she clearly heard words like "will you fetch me some beer," as if Mrs. Godman entertained a visitor in her bedchamber. Then, one hot day when Mrs. Godman returned home from a walk and retired to her room, the girls decided to spy on her. They climbed up to the attic, to a spot directly above Mrs. Godman's room, where they could peer through the floorboards. There they saw Mrs. Godman in bed, partially clothed, behaving as if someone (the Devil?) might be under the covers with her. The girls called down to Mrs. Godman: "What have you there?" Mrs. Godman, angry and indignant, insisted that she was alone, and she threatened to punish the girls for invading her privacy. Two days later, one of the girls "heard a hideous noise," felt someone pinching her, and fell into a "dreadful fit" and fever. Was this Mrs. Godman's revenge?

With testimony so lurid, Mrs. Godman had no chance of winning her defamation case. Governor Eaton and the panel of judges, which included Stephen Goodyear, found that Mrs. Godman's "carriage doth justly render her suspicious of witchcraft" and warned that they would continue watching her. They ordered her to "meddle with her own business," and to stop going "to folks' houses in a rayling manner."

Mrs. Godman returned to the Goodyear house, but she did not remain docile for long. Two years later her old accusers (and some new ones) renewed the witchcraft charges, and Mrs. Godman was back in court. Goodwife Thorpe, who had previously blamed Mrs. Godman for the death of chickens, now believed that her cows suffered harm when Mrs. Godman "gnashed and grinned with her teeth in a strange manner." Allen Ball's pigs died—and Mr. Hooke's beer spoiled—after similar encounters with a "muttering" and "discontented" Mrs. Godman.

But it was the Goodyear daughters, again, who offered the most dramatic testimony. One night the girls were "awakened with a great fumbling at the chamber door." *Something* came into their room. "It came nearer the bed and Hanah was afraid and called father, but he heard not, which made her more afraid." Then the intruder pulled at the bedcovers; the girls held on, and a tug-of-war ensued, which "frighted them so that Hanah Goodyeare called her father so loud as . . . might be heard to the meeting-house." The mysterious prowler had disappeared by the time Stephen Goodyear arrived on the scene, but Mrs. Godman, of course, was the prime suspect.

Mrs. Godman never managed to clear her name, but she escaped the gallows; the judges decided that the evidence was "not sufficient . . . to take away her life." The Goodyears, however, evicted Mrs. Godman from her upstairs room. Despite community concerns, she stayed in New Haven, and Thomas Johnson's family (apparently brave enough to risk associating with a suspected witch) took her in. She faced no further witchcraft charges, and she spent the rest of her life (five more years) in the Johnson household. Perhaps she simply learned to keep quiet and avoid offense—or maybe she finally found a family where an outspoken woman could feel at home.

WATCHING WIDOW HOLMAN

On June 21, 1659, the thirty-seven-year-old magistrate Thomas Danforth dipped his quill into an ink pot and penned a few short sentences on a small piece of paper, one of his first official acts as a newly elected judge in the Massachusetts Bay Colony. The document he signed was a warrant to arrest his own neighbors, people he had known for nearly twenty-five years: "To the Constable of Cambridge. You are required forthwith to apprehend the persons of Widow Holman and her daughter Mary, and immediately bring them before the County Court now sitting at Charlestown, to be examined on several accusations presented, on suspicion of witchcraft."

Witchcraft was a capital crime, such a serious matter that Danforth decided to take special precautions. He instructed the constable to seize mother and daughter separately: "Charge some meet person to bring away the maid first," he suggested, "and then you may acquaint the mother also with this warrant." Undoubtedly, Danforth wanted to ensure that the women could not plan their testimony together before they were questioned, but he also may have worried about the logistics of apprehending two suspected witches —would they use their diabolical powers to resist arrest or to flee? And Danforth apparently had yet another reason to handle this case carefully;

Rebecca Stearns, the Holmans' chief accuser, told her parents that "Mr. Danforth was chosen a magistrate to find out Mrs. Holman." For a young and earnest Puritan magistrate, this was a heady start to his judicial career.

Danforth also summoned as witnesses John Gibson and his wife, again cautioning the constable to ensure that the Gibsons could not influence each other's testimony: "You are forthwith to bring them away, and not suffer them to speak one with another after their knowledge of this warrant, and hereof you are not to fail at your peril." These witnesses, as well as the accused Holman women, would be questioned by a panel of judges (not just Danforth)—and perhaps by a grand jury of local citizens—at the tavern in Charlestown, Massachusetts, where the Middlesex County Court was in session. Danforth already had a good idea of what the Gibsons would say in court, however, for they were the reason that he signed the arrest warrant. This distraught and desperate couple had sought him out, probably at his mansion house in Cambridge, with a story so troubling that Danforth recorded it verbatim in pages of copious notes.

The Gibsons and the Holmans—like Danforth—had been Cambridge neighbors since the mid-1630s, among the earliest immigrants from England to the Massachusetts Bay Colony. As Danforth was well aware, John Gibson and his wife had raised five children in a house northwest of the Cambridge Common (on the south side of what is now Garden Street). William and Winifred Holman, with their children, lived across the road. When the Gibsons' eldest daughter, Rebecca, married in 1654, she and her husband, Charles Stearns, moved next door to Rebecca's parents. Although that part of Cambridge was not densely populated, much of the land had been cleared for farming and meadow, so the Gibson, Stearns, and Holman houses stood in plain view of each other—and, as in small towns everywhere, these neighbors watched each other's activities with curiosity. They were not close friends, but their physical proximity meant near-daily interaction (and sometimes annoyance). John Gibson complained, for example, that the Holman chickens would not stay on their side of the road, coming over to eat corn in the Gibson barn. And the eldest Holman daughter, Mary, walked to the Gibsons' almost every morning with a skillet to "borrow fire," since the Holmans somehow could not manage (unlike the Gibsons) to keep their hearth fire burning day and night.

By about January 1659, when serious troubles began, Mrs. Holman was a widow in her sixties, living with her eldest children, Mary (about thirty years old) and Abraham (in his twenties). At least one child still lived in the Gibson household, John Gibson Jr., a teenager, but much of the Gibson family's attention was focused on their married daughter, Rebecca Stearns, who suffered from mysterious fits and hysterical outbursts. Doctors had been unable to help. One day, after Rebecca experienced "two extraordinary strange fits," Mary walked across the road and suggested that her mother could offer a cure. Apparently, Mary and her mother were known in the community as healers—many New England women dispensed home remedies, nursed sick neighbors, and assisted at childbirths—and Goody Gibson urged her daughter "to go and to see what [Mrs. Holman] would say." Mrs. Holman prescribed some herbs that Rebecca "should use in the spring."

Then, before Rebecca could begin the herbal therapy, her baby fell ill. Mary, "coming in often" to Rebecca's house, diagnosed the problem as rickets, predicting that the child would continue to decline and "come to the grave but if you will put it into my hands I will undertake to cure it." She pointed out that she had "cured one at Malden that had the rickets," and even the Cambridge minister's child had been cured of the same disease by "a skillful woman." But Rebecca could not decide what to do about her child. Mary, evidently frustrated and convinced that the baby would die without treatment, told Rebecca, "You will take a fool's counsel . . . if you will not choose."

After that, Rebecca's fits began again—first "ordinary fits 2 nights and 2 days," and then, after being "pretty well again and sensible one day . . . she was taken with a strange raving . . . for 3 or 4 days." Goody Gibson, frantic with worry as she tried to care for her disturbed daughter and sick grandchild, happened to look across the road during one of Rebecca's rages. She noticed that "Mrs. Holman was walking about by her rails stooping down and picking of the ground along as she went" (looking for healing plants and herbs?). As Rebecca's condition changed, day to day, hour to hour, Goody Gibson continued watching the Holmans. Whenever Mrs. Holman or Mary Holman walked along their rail fence, Rebecca "raged [and] could not be quiet," but when the Holman women were away, Rebecca slept peacefully. One afternoon Rebecca suddenly sprang up from a sound sleep "and cried out with . . . rage against Mrs. Holman that she was a witch and that she must be hanged." At that very moment, Goody Gibson looked outside and was amazed to see Mrs. Holman walking toward the house.

The next morning, when Mary Holman arrived at the door, as usual, to "borrow fire," Rebecca screamed hysterically, saying that Mary was a witch, too. When Mary came for fire the next day, the same thing happened. On the third day, the Gibsons turned Mary away and "bade her go to some other house" for fire. They also began to keep constant watch on the Holman house across the road, trying to figure out a cause-and-effect relationship between the Holmans' activities and the health of Rebecca and her baby. Perhaps the Gibsons kept a daily journal, because they reported their observations to Danforth in surprising detail.

The Gibsons noticed countless strange things that Widow Holman did, in addition to picking along the fence. They "observed that the old woman [was] seen to go out toward night into swamps and highways," and sometimes Mrs. Holman walked in the rain for no apparent reason. They saw Mrs. Holman kneeling in her yard, digging with a hoe for hours, but later when Goody Gibson went over to look, she "could . . . see no hole at all more than in any other place at the spot." Once, when the Gibsons looked at the house across the road, they saw "a great heap of sand" at the Holmans' door, and then the widow "began to carry it away in a great dish." An unusual white bird flew around the Holman house at night, "too late for birds to be abroad." And many of these strange things seemed to coincide with Rebecca's fits and rages. For example, Rebecca's father described one time when his daughter cried uncontrollably, "the tears [falling] so fast from her eyes that my wife was fain to stand and wipe them off her face with her apron," and they looked outside to see Mrs. Holman pouring water from one container to another.

Rebecca's outbursts grew more frequent and horrifying. She "barked like a dog" during prayers; she writhed about in bed, trembling and shaking, crying out that she "fought with the Devil"; she claimed that a huge snake "stung her under her arms" and that "imps" from Mrs. Holman's black chest bit her feet. The few times when Rebecca went out in public, she loudly accused Widow Holman and her daughter, saying that they "were witches and bewitched her and her child." And, as Mary Holman had predicted,

Rebecca's baby did "decline and fall away daily, . . . quite crooked in the body which before was a straight thriving child."

Rebecca's parents reported all these observations to Thomas Danforth, and much, much more—Danforth filled pages of notes with their testimony. Presumably, the Gibsons repeated this strange story at the court in Charlestown. But what happened next is not clear. There is no record that the Holmans ever faced trial for witchcraft. Most likely, the grand jury (or the judges presiding with Danforth) simply did not believe that the Gibsons' testimony was sufficient to support a witchcraft indictment, and they sent everybody home. The Gibsons and the Holmans returned to their uneasy relationship, watching each other from across the road.

The Gibsons, however, remained wary, and Rebecca continued accusing the Holmans of witchcraft. Even Rebecca's brother John joined in the witch-craft talk, telling his friends when he saw Mary Holman, "There cometh the young witch."

Finally, the Holman women could bear the suspicion no longer. In March 1660 Mrs. Holman sued Rebecca Stearns, her parents, and John Gibson Jr. for defamation and slander. (Tellingly, Mrs. Holman bypassed her town magistrate, Thomas Danforth, who ordinarily would receive the complaint and sign the court papers. Instead, a court clerk, Samuel Green, signed writs summoning the defendants.) And, in an unprecedented show of sup-port, twenty-five longtime neighbors (including some of Cambridge's most respected citizens) submitted a petition attesting to Mrs. Holman's good character and affirming that they "never knew anything in her life concern-ing witchery."

When the case came to trial in April 1660, Thomas Danforth was one of four men at the judges' table. The jury returned a verdict for John Gibson and his wife, apparently because the couple did not actually *say* that the Holmans were witches. Rebecca Stearns, however, clearly accused Winifred and Mary Holman of witchcraft many times, but the jury decided that Rebecca "was by God's hand deprived of her natural reason when she expressed those words"—mentally incompetent to be responsible for her statements. So that left John Gibson Jr., who had no good excuse (except the rashness of youth) for calling Mary Holman a witch. The court convicted him of slander but let him off with the choice of paying a five-pound fine or giving Mary an apology. He stood up in court to recite this little speech (perhaps drafted for him by Thomas Danforth): I am "heartily sorry for [my] evil thereby committed against God, and wrong done to . . . Mary Holman and her friends, and [I] . . . crave forgiveness of the said Mary Holman of this trespass."

The result was as close to vindication as Widow Holman would ever get. After that, the Holmans and the Gibson and Stearns families went back to being neighbors, still living in houses where they had to look at each other every day from across the road. Maybe the Gibsons allowed Mary to "borrow fire" again. Perhaps Rebecca's fits subsided—did she finally try the herbs that Mrs. Holman prescribed?—for she moved away to nearby Watertown with her husband, Charles. No one ever accused the Holman women of witchcraft again. And Thomas Danforth, whose judicial career started with a witchcraft scare, faced hard decisions about accused witches once more near the end of his life (see chapter 10)—as a judge at the Salem witchcraft trials.

Writ issued by the court clerk, Samuel Green, in Widow Holman's slander case.

A WOMAN OF "ENTHUSIASTICAL POWER"

In the summer of 1683 a shocking crime came to trial in Plymouth Colony. Judges heard how a vagrant couple—a married man and his young female consort—terrorized a local family in a brutal home invasion. This unusual case must have been the talk of the colony—in every tavern, at Sunday meeting, anyplace where people gathered to share the news—yet the event soon faded from historical memory. No newspapers reported the case, and little remains to tell the tale, except for a cryptic summary of evidence in the court records.

The accused man called himself Jonathan Dunham, but he also used an alias—Shingleterry or Singletary—and the Plymouth authorities had encountered him before. "For some considerable time," according to the court records, Jonathan Dunham "hath been wandering about from place to place as a vagabond in this colony, also disseminating his corrupt principles." In the parlance of the 1600s, "corrupt principles" could only mean that Jonathan was an itinerant preacher, probably Quaker or Baptist, whose sermons were unwelcome in Plymouth Colony. Even worse than his religious beliefs, Jonathan's behavior suggested loose morals, if not outright adultery. As the court pointed out, he "hath long absented himself from his wife and family," ignoring warnings to return home, and "drawing away another mans wife," who followed Jonathan "against her husband's consent."

What happened to the other man's wife is not clear, but Jonathan apparently left her for a younger female companion—Mary Rosse. Perhaps Mary shared Jonathan's passion for preaching; maybe she was one of the bold and charismatic Quaker women who traveled throughout New England advocating religious freedom. Or it is possible that Jonathan simply could not resist her personal charms. As Jonathan described their relationship, he followed Mary, doing whatever she told him to do, "led by [her] enthusiastical power."

For some reason, Mary led Jonathan to the house of John Irish at Little Compton, Rhode Island (then part of the Plymouth Colony). The events that followed can only be described as bizarre, but neither Mary nor Jonathan denied the charges. First they entered the house and killed John Irish's dog. Then, when the outraged Irish tried to force the couple out, they refused to leave. "According to their anticke tricks and foolish powers,"

Jonathan and Mary "made a fire in the said house, and threw the dog upon it, and shot of a gun several times, and burnt some other things in the house." Somehow Irish ended up outside the burning home, his young children trapped inside with Jonathan and Mary, who had barred the doors. The frantic father managed to summon help from his neighbors and rescue the children, while authorities took the couple into custody.

Invading and burning another man's home, killing the family dog, and threatening the lives of small children were serious offenses, but the Plymouth authorities had no interest in keeping Jonathan and Mary locked up in prison. Apparently worried more about the duo's controversial religious views than their violent actions, the court ordered banishment. Jonathan was "publicly whipped at the post," and then "required . . . to depart forth with out of this colony," with threats of further whipping and expulsion "as oft as he shall . . . return . . . to disseminate his corrupt principles." Mary expressed no contrition—treating the judges to "uncivil and outrageous railing words and carriages"—so she received an even harsher punishment. Sentenced to forcible removal, Mary suffered multiple whippings while "conveyed from constable to constable out of this government towards Boston, where her mother dwells."

Here the official court record trails off, leaving us with more questions than answers. Who were these people—the enigmatic Mary Rosse and the vagabond Jonathan Dunham-Singletary, who could not resist her "enthusiastical power"? Where did they come from? What happened after Plymouth forced the couple out of the colony?

Mary's origins remain uncertain, although the court records state that her mother lived in Boston. Her father was likely one of the Scottish soldiers captured during the English Civil War and exiled to colonial servitude during the mid-1600s. Jonathan's background is easier to trace, from his birth in 1639 at Salisbury, Massachusetts, the eldest son of Richard Singletary. Family lore hints that Richard Singletary really was a Dunham—heir to an English fortune—who fled to America when rivals plotted his murder. Those fanciful allegations cannot be substantiated, but we do know that Richard's son, Jonathan Singletary, grew up in Haverhill, Massachusetts, and married a local woman, Mary Bloomfield.

Whipping at the Cart's Tayle.

Essex County records suggest an ordinary life for Jonathan Singletary and no trace of the religious zeal or instability that shaped his later years, except for one peculiar brush with the supernatural. In 1662 Jonathan landed in an Ipswich jail cell for failing (or refusing) to pay debts owed to his neighbor John Godfrey. Alone in the dark, late at night, Jonathan was startled by "a great Noise as if many Cats had been Climbing up" the prison walls, "stools had been thrown about, & men walking in ye Chambers & a Crackling & Shaking as if ye house would have fallen upon me." The noises frightened Jonathan, but not as much as the spectral figure of Godfrey, who suddenly seemed to materialize inside the locked prison chamber. When released from jail, Jonathan accused Godfrey of witchcraft, which prompted Godfrey to sue for defamation.

Jonathan lost the defamation case, and not long afterward he moved with his wife's family to Woodbridge, New Jersey. There, perhaps to make a fresh start, or to reclaim his ancestral heritage, Jonathan began using the surname Dunham. He acquired land, raised a family, and became a respectable miller, until Quakers began settling nearby. In the late 1670s Jonathan—apparently motivated by Quaker fervor or a midlife crisis—broke into the governor's house, abandoned his wife and family, and reinvented himself as a peripatetic preacher, finally coming under the spell of the "enthusiastical" Mary Rosse.

What Jonathan and Mary did immediately after their 1683 expulsion from Plymouth is unknown, but they both appeared in Woodbridge, New Jersey, six years later. Perhaps their relationship had run its course, for Jonathan returned to his wife and children, and he remained with them for the rest of his life. But here the story takes a curious twist. Somehow Mary Rosse persuaded Jonathan to deed his Woodbridge house and land to her. Then she moved in and began an affair with another New Jersey man, James Seaton, who had recently separated from his pregnant wife.

Although James was not legally divorced, he and Mary made no secret of their liaison. Many neighbors reported seeing the couple in bed together. James boasted "that Mary Rosse was his Wife and that she was a Whore, and that he . . . had carnal knowledge of her body more than a hundred times." Finally, in 1693 Seaton's legal wife sued for abandonment and adultery and obtained a divorce, which was rare for seventeenth-century New Jersey. Mary and James escaped before they could be punished. Safely outside the jurisdiction, Mary reconveyed the Woodbridge property to her old companion Jonathan and made a new life for herself—this time in New York. Undoubtedly, her "enthusiastical power" remained as strong as ever.

Chapter 2

COUPLING

Puritan prohibitions could not curb sexual attraction. Many New Englanders landed in court for premarital dalliance, adultery, and other acts of love and lust. Although it is difficult to choose—the court records offer so many stories about seventeenth-century couples who could not keep their hands off each other—the following three stories are typical.

"The Scottish Rogue" takes us to a Connecticut ironworks village where a young man defends himself against charges of sexual misconduct. In "The Wandering Wife," a teenage girl attracts and marries an older man but finds herself not ready to settle down. The final story in this chapter, "The Rhode Island Runaway," is a poignant look at a doomed love affair and the unexpected redemption that follows.

THE SCOTTISH ROGUE

The word *rogue* sounds quaintly comic to the modern ear, a seldom-used term more likely to provoke laughter than indignation. In seventeenth-century New England, however, calling someone a rogue was no joke. Rogue meant liar, villain, or scoundrel—usually with a hint of sexual misbehavior—and it was the worst sort of insult, liable to trigger a fistfight or a slander suit. Accused rogues often wound up explaining themselves to a judge or jury, and the court records reveal amusing—and sometimes shocking—details of life in long-ago New England. One case from colonial New Haven offers a particularly colorful glimpse into the bawdy culture of a Connecticut ironworks village, where a Scotsman, Patrick Morran, feuded with the Pinion family.

When Patrick first arrived in Massachusetts with a shipload of Scottish war prisoners in 1652, he occupied one of the lowest rungs on the Puritan social ladder, little better than a slave. (Apparently, he was one of the Scots captured in 1651 by Oliver Cromwell's troops at the Battle of Worcester, near the end of the English Civil War.) As servant to Oliver Purchase, clerk of the Hammersmith Ironworks in Lynn, Patrick became acquainted with the family of a carpenter, Nicholas Pinion. Pinion was no gentleman—his penchant for drunken violence often landed him in court—but he worked for wages at Hammersmith and had enough clout to "rent" Scotsmen from the ironworks company. By the mid-1600s, Patrick and Nicholas had found new work at a small forge along East Haven's Furnace Pond (today's Lake Saltonstall in Connecticut). The move brought a curious role reversal for the two men. Patrick had earned his freedom and was beginning a career as clerk-paymaster of the East Haven ironworks, his astonishing good fortune probably due to literacy, bookkeeping skills, and good relations with his former master. Nicholas and his family now found themselves uncomfortably subordinate to Patrick, forced to take their orders, and wages, from a former Scottish servant.

Soon the Pinion women were calling Patrick a "Scotch rogue," but whether he deserved the epithet is difficult to judge. The surviving court evidence suggests a Pinion vendetta against the Scottish ironworks clerk, but Patrick's own poor judgment surely contributed to his legal troubles. Sorting out the truth was not easy for the New Haven magistrates when Patrick went on trial in January 1665, accused by Elizabeth Pinion of "attempting to Violate the Chastity of [her] two daughters."

Fifteen-year-old Hannah Pinion furnished lurid testimony. "One rainy day," Patrick followed Hannah on an errand and offered her a pair of gloves, "if she would come to the furnace with him and let him lie with her." Hannah rejected this proposition, telling Patrick that she would not do what he asked "for many gloves." Patrick persisted, promising to wait for her at the ironworks and to leave a signal on the furnace bridge. Three weeks later, Patrick allegedly tried again, raising the stakes by offering Hannah gloves and a pair of stockings, his new signal to be "a great stone . . . upon the black stump by the house." She still refused. When Hannah went to Patrick's room one Friday night—purportedly to ask him for a pound of sugar—he sweetened the offer of gloves with a silver shilling, too, if she would lie with him. Apparently sure of success this time, he brandished the shilling, took her in his arms, and flung her on the bed, but she threatened "if he would not be quiet she would call out to the folk below, and so he set her down again."

Elizabeth Pinion supported her daughter's testimony, recounting several times when she sent Hannah to the company store (which Patrick managed) for items such as gloves, stockings, liquor, or sugar, and Hannah returned home empty-handed. Patrick would not dispense these goods, Hannah told her, unless he could "have the use of her body in an unclean way."

Ruth Moore, Hannah's older sister, also testified. When she learned from Hannah "how Patricke inticed her," Ruth arranged to stop by the forge on one of the appointed nights herself, taking the precaution of asking a neighbor, Thomas Luddington, to follow her to observe what might happen. Ruth found Patrick standing at the shop door by the furnace bridge, and after some teasing banter, she accepted his invitation to "drink a dram of the bottle." Then he invited Ruth into the shop, making such "immodest and shameful" suggestions that Ruth was "ashamed to speak [of] it" in court. According to Ruth, only Luddington's arrival on the scene prevented Patrick from taking improper advantage.

When the next witness took the stand, however, the case against Patrick began to unravel. Nicholas Pinion spoke in surprisingly neutral terms for a father whose daughters claimed to be the victims of unwanted sexual advances. Nicholas emphasized that he had no complaint against Patrick—in fact, he had discouraged his wife's lawsuit—and he described a congenial relationship with Patrick as a drinking partner and a visitor to their home. Thomas Luddington did not exactly corroborate Ruth's testimony, either, when his turn came to testify. Although he had tried to follow Ruth to the forge, she had hurried on ahead, and halfway there he found Patrick escorting Ruth homeward. Patrick expressed concern about being seen "with this woman . . . of such an ill report," and he asked Thomas not to "make it known, for it would be a scandal to the gospel and a Blemish to his name."

The judges finally asked Patrick for his side of the story, and he insisted that he was innocent. He denied offering Hannah gloves or silver, leaving signals, or making "any such attempt" on her honor. He admitted asking Ruth to visit the forge on the night in question, but only to talk with her on behalf of a jilted friend who felt that "she had done him wrong." Goody Pinion and her

daughters falsely accused him, Patrick believed, because "he would not let the old woman have so much Commodities as she desired." He testified about one occasion when he had refused to give Elizabeth the blue linen she demanded (apparently because she had overextended her credit at the company store). She "abused him with her tongue and took up an axe . . . and called him Scotch dog and Scotch Rogue and said she would knock him down."

Questioned by the judges about the axe-wielding incident, Elizabeth confessed that it was true. The court had heard enough and ruled in Patrick's favor—he was "not . . . such a person as they accuse him to be"—but the verdict stopped short of exoneration. Patrick "hath imprudently carried it," the court declared, which "renders him suspicious of something of the like nature."

Not content to walk away with a lukewarm victory, Patrick filed a slander suit against the Pinion women, seeking the enormous sum of two hundred pounds. When the judges asked Patrick the basis for his large damage claim, he pointed out that the Pinions had ruined his good name, and that "he esteemed his name above . . . money." The court's arch response, "that he might over Esteem his name," did not bode well for a huge recovery. Patrick won his case—he proved defamation—but the award was a paltry five pounds, with fifty shillings for court costs.

Patrick's tangled relations with the Pinion family continued to keep the courts busy. A Pinion son broke into the ironworks storehouse, vandalizing Patrick's ledger and stealing rum, sugar, stockings, and gunpowder. Patrick scuffled with Nicholas Pinion at the forge, and Elizabeth stole the Scotsman's blanket. Patrick successfully deflected new accusations of "unsuitable and unseasonable familiarity" with Hannah, and of sexual relations with Ruth (who later was hanged in Hartford for infanticide and adultery), but the judges warned him to be "wary . . . of being in privacy with such persons as those." Death threats in 1671 finally convinced Patrick to quit the East Haven job. He returned to Massachusetts, reduced to low-level work as another man's servant.

Patrick's troubles did not end with the Pinions out of his life. By 1672 he had provoked Massachusetts women to call him "a naughty man" and accuse him of harassment, perhaps validating Goody Pinion's assessment—that he was, indeed, a "Scotch rogue." Soon Patrick, as a soldier in King Philip's War, was fending off Indians instead of angry women, and he disappeared from history.

THE WANDERING WIFE

In 1675 Faith Black lived on a farm in Topsfield, Massachusetts, with her husband, Daniel, and five young children, who ranged in age from ten-year-old Margrett to newborn Edmond. Near their modest home, probably located in present-day Boxford, Daniel supplemented the family income as a woodcutter at the Rowley Village ironworks.

Goodwife Black seemed a model of propriety. When one of the ironworkers used foul language, she chastised him "for talking so vilely," and she testified in court against a neighbor who "behaved very uncivilly." Faith Black, however, had not always been a paragon of virtue. Only a few years earlier, she and Daniel had roiled the community with scandals of their own, and the seventeenth-century Essex County Court records preserve the story in remarkable detail.

The problems began before their marriage, when Faith's father, Edmond Bridges, learned that his fourteen-year-old daughter was carrying on with a man more than twice her age. Bridges feared that matters already had progressed too far, and he complained to the magistrates about this man of "notorious evil carriage," Daniel Black, who had stolen his daughter's affections. Since courting a woman without her parents' permission was a crime in Puritan Massachusetts, the authorities issued a warrant for Daniel's arrest. The case was heard in Ipswich Quarterly Court, probably at a local tavern, in September 1660.

Interrogated by the magistrates, Faith and Daniel confessed. They had met secretly over the summer. Once, in an act of surprising boldness, Faith smuggled Daniel into her own house for a nighttime rendezvous "late upon the last day of June, 1660, when the family were in bed." Daniel engineered another tryst, enlisting an Irish servant friend to bring a bottle of wine and "to draw the said young wench to him" at an Ipswich house while the occupants were away.

Such immorality could not go unpunished, although Faith was too young to be legally culpable, and the damage to her reputation may have seemed penalty enough. Thirty-two-year-old Daniel, however, was fined the hefty sum of five pounds "for making love to the daughter of Edmond Bridges without consent of her parents." Unable to pay, Daniel apparently remained in prison, but he sent an intermediary to Faith's father, hinting at a deal that "may do well on both parties." Negotiations must have succeeded, for Daniel's fine was "respitted," which suggests a compromise that gained Daniel his freedom and salvaged Faith's honor. The next time Faith appeared in the court records, her name was Goodwife Black.

Daniel acquired a house and land from Faith's brother, and he worked to support his teenage bride, but Faith was not ready to settle down as a Topsfield housewife. She flirted openly with other men. She neglected her chores, leaving the cow unmilked, the hogs unfed, the clothes unwashed— and no food on the table for Daniel when he returned to the house after a long day's labor. She spent more time away than at home, visiting friends or loitering at the tavern, and some nights she failed to return from her wanderings. Neighbors saw Faith walking alone at dusk with Judah Trumble; others reported that she kept frequent company with the married John How and shared his bed. Daniel cursed and argued, cajoled and threatened, but Faith refused to mend her ways

In an era when men were expected to discipline their wives, it would not have been surprising if Daniel had resorted to physical abuse, but there is little evidence that his anger went much beyond words. Yet Daniel had his breaking point, and finally, after one absence too many, he took action. This time when Faith returned home, he refused to let her back in the house. He "told her to go and shift for herself and pulled off her stockings," leaving Faith to walk "half a mile up to the knees in snow" to a neighbor's house.

Faith, with her brother's backing, filed a complaint against Daniel "for having forced his wife from him, not suffering her to live with him." Daniel, who apparently could write, penned a long tirade in his own defense, describing himself as "a pore man . . . that hath nothing to live by but his labor," and detailing not only Faith's infidelities but the financial losses caused by her wifely neglect.

At the Ipswich court session in September 1664, magistrates and jurymen weighed the testimony of Faith and Daniel, and of their neighbors, family, and friends. Almost everyone in Topsfield seemed to have an opinion about the turbulent Blacks, many telling of Daniel's jealousy and threats. John How, for example, testified that he heard Daniel "wish god to damn his soul if he did not Beat his wife's Brains out."

Other witnesses, however, supported Daniel. Thomas Hobbs and his wife, his neighbors, admired Daniel's long-suffering patience, pointing out that "a woman ought to be a meet help for a man," but that Faith's behavior "was not fitting for any woman." She "provoke[d] him both by her tongue and carriages," the Hobbs couple testified. They had heard Daniel say:

> that if his wife would stay at home, dress his victuals and
> wash his clothes and do by him as by a husband, he would
> allow her time to see her friends as much as she desired. But
> when she had been out two or three days and nights together,
> he could not help speaking to her. . . .When he reproved
> her, she said she would do it again. If [Goodwife Hobbs] had
> not washed his clothes and fed his swine, they would have
> suffered, yet all the thanks Black's wife gave . . . was to tell
> her that she did not ask her to do it.

Even Faith's own brother conceded "that his sister . . . might live as well with Daniel . . . as any poor woman in Topsfield, but her proud spirit was enough to provoke anyone to do things that he would not do at another time."

The court found blame on both sides and resolved the case with a unique joint punishment: Faith and Daniel *both* were sentenced to one hour in the stocks—together—with warnings against future misconduct. Daniel "was not to threaten his wife or miscall her and to live peaceably with her, and she was to be orderly and not to gad abroad . . . or be in company with John How or Judah Trumble nor come to the house of John How unless her husband sent her on business." If either of them "offended against this order, they were to be whipped."

Several months later, at a court session in Ipswich, "Daniell Black was sentenced to be whipped or pay a fine," so he may have lost his temper one more time, although the court files offer no detail. By October 1665 the couple's first child was born, followed by four more over the next decade. Faith and Daniel must have resolved their differences and settled down to a peaceful family life, because the courts never again found cause to intervene in their marriage. Perhaps parenting brought a new appreciation for each other; perhaps Faith simply grew up. Whatever the reason, Faith had matured by the 1670s into the role of respectable goodwife, passing judgment on the misbehavior of her neighbors.

THE RHODE ISLAND RUNAWAY

On a cold day late in 1670, a couple on horseback arrived at the ferry land-ing in Charlestown, Massachusetts. The man dismounted and reached up to help a young woman, Mary Ball, who rode pillion behind the saddle. They walked to the water's edge and paid the fare. Perhaps another passenger, with a squealing pig or a crate of chickens, shifted to make room while Mary boarded the boat. Mary's companion, however, returned to his horse and watched from shore as the ferryman rowed across the Charles River to Boston.

Mary was running away. At Boston Harbor she would find the first ship sail-ing for Rhode Island—a fishing boat, merchant bark, any vessel willing to transport a lone woman traveler. Her flight triggered a scandal and a notori-ous court case, yet the incident finally faded from memory, forgotten or deliberately suppressed by later generations. Mary's story might have van-ished from history, had not the Massachusetts Archives preserved the court records—some in Mary's own words. Those files are incomplete, scattered on microfilm reels and in boxes of folio papers, but they reveal a lost tale of troubled seventeenth-century lives.

Eighteen years before that desperate voyage to Rhode Island, Mary began life in Watertown, Massachusetts, born to John Ball, a tailor, and his wife, Elizabeth. John Ball, who apparently craved more adventure than a tailor's shop could offer, worked his way forty miles west, clearing land and trading with Indians at the frontier "plantation" of Lancaster. John had his in-laws' approval (Elizabeth's father, John Peirce, a Watertown weaver, invested in the new town), and John must have returned to his wife on occasion (the family grew—there were at least three more daughters after Mary), but John's name rarely appears in Watertown records.

John's prolonged absences strained the marriage, and Elizabeth suffered from illness or depression—or perhaps she voiced complaints unseemly for a Puritan goodwife. The family reached a breaking point, and Watertown officials intervened, ordering an investigation "into the estate of Sister Ball" and requiring John Ball to appear at a town meeting "to make known his condition." Mary's grandparents took permanent custody of five-year-old Mary and her older brother, promising to train the boy as a weaver and to teach both children how to "read the English tongue." Other Watertown citizens fostered the younger children at John Ball's expense.

But Mary's family remained in crisis. In 1657 and 1658 the Middlesex County Court convicted Elizabeth of "disorderly carriages" toward her neighbors and husband, and even a shocking fistfight with her elderly father. The judges warned that Elizabeth's "distempered mind" posed dangers for the entire community, and that Watertown must be vigilant to thwart "Satan's temptation." Elizabeth countered, however, with accusations of "hard usage" and mistreatment, saying that John "had not only neglected her, in suffering her to want necessary supplies, but also had kicked her." John admitted beating his wife, but he received no punishment; Watertown's minister pleaded for clemency, saying that the church was dealing with the matter. The court merely admonished John to live with his wife "according to Gods Holy word & Rules" and "to use her kindly."

Maybe John and Elizabeth tried living together again, but Elizabeth soon died. John remarried and sold the family farm in Watertown, apparently renting property in Lancaster and moving there with his young bride. Both of Mary's grandparents died, too, and sixteen-year-old Mary was put out to service with a family near her uncle's farm in Woburn.

Mary's young master, Michael Bacon Jr. (whom we will meet again in chapter 6) presided over a multigenerational household: his wife, Sarah (who also was his stepsister), their several small children, and Michael's aging father and stepmother. If the court records are any indication, the Bacon men were volatile and quarrelsome, constantly suing or being sued over wandering livestock, broken contracts, land titles, slander, forgery; the list goes on and on. But Michael Bacon must have possessed a certain charm, for his servant Mary soon was smitten—and pregnant.

They panicked. Mary's condition could not be concealed for long, especially from Michael's wife, who was pregnant again herself, or from the town constable, who would arrest the illicit lovers. Legal sanctions were inevitable. (Technically, the offense was fornication—not the capital crime of adultery, since Mary was unmarried—but Massachusetts zealously prosecuted fornicators and imposed punishments ranging from fines, whippings, public humiliation, to imprisonment.) Mary must leave before her preg-

Bastardy bond of Michael Bacon, 1671,
"to sattisfy all ye charges arising for the bringing up of ye child of Mary Ball."

nancy became obvious, but where to go? Neighboring Rhode Island, known for laissez-faire tolerance, was the destination of choice for many colonists fleeing harsh Massachusetts laws. Mary had tenuous family connections in Rhode Island; her Watertown cousin Joseph Peirce had married a Brayton woman from Portsmouth, whose parents still lived there. But what next? How could Mary support herself and a child? Michael made promises to send money, perhaps even to leave his wife and join Mary in Rhode Island. He made a furtive trip with Mary, as far as the Charlestown ferry, then rode back to his farm and family.

Somehow Mary found passage from Boston to Portsmouth, Rhode Island. Francis Brayton and his wife welcomed her as a temporary houseguest; seventeenth-century etiquette mandated such hospitality when unexpected friends or relatives, no matter how distant, arrived at the door. Mary must have offered some plausible explanation for the visit, while she waited anxiously for Michael—and days stretched into weeks, until finally she could hide the pregnancy no longer. She confessed "that the child she went with was begotten by Michael Bacon . . . and by no other man."

Francis Brayton traveled back to Massachusetts with a letter for Michael—signed by Mary—a plea from "one in distress" to "you who . . . have stationed my travails unto a strange place where my shame is not a little." Mary begged her former master not to forget his promises. "You only on Earth knows how things were at the first with us." But Michael denied responsibility, and Brayton turned the letter over to court authorities. The long-absent

John Ball pressed charges against Michael "for carrying Mary . . . out of the jurisdiction without her father's order."

Michael landed in prison, but, incredibly, he escaped, running off "in ye woods." Judge Thomas Danforth issued a hue and cry, ordering constables "to make pursuit & search for him." (Danforth made his first appearance here in chapter 1; he will reappear in chapters 3, 6, and 10.) Local men who had been deputized to apprehend the fugitive "watched the bridges all night" in Cambridge and Watertown, and a few days later Michael was back in custody. He appeared in court, promising to support Mary's child and to post a "bastardy bond." Mary returned from Rhode Island (apparently with her child, who was born en route), petitioning the court with a plaintive plea for leniency. "I would not so much blame my master as my own heart," she said, "but there is no place free from temptation."

Michael returned to his wife, Sarah, fathering at least six more children and maturing into a respectable citizen. Mary, too, found a new chance at happiness, with ten more children (and four stepchildren), married to a Cambridge Scotsman, William Munro (who reappears in chapter 6). But what was the fate of Mary's first child? Bacon, Ball, and Munro genealogies do not mention him. I am still searching, although I believe that I have found the child in a surprising source. But until I can solve that genealogical puzzle, the child's story must wait—perhaps for a future book of true New England tales.

Chapter 3

PARENTS AND YOUTH

Young people defied authority, broke rules, and partied with friends in colonial New England, just as they do today, and rebellious or rowdy behavior often resulted in court intervention. The stories in this chapter, however, tell what happened when the Puritan legal authorities almost went too far in enforcing their strict moral codes.

"The Prodigal Son" looks at the tragically dysfunctional Porter family of Salem Village, Massachusetts, and a father-son conflict that spanned decades. The second story, "Dancing in the 'Night Season,'" reveals furtive merrymaking—and a surprising guest list—at a series of parties in and around Harvard College in the late seventeenth century.

THE PRODIGAL SON

When John Porter left London in the 1650s, on a ship bound for New England, he needed faith and courage to endure what lay ahead. Seventeenth-century ocean travel could take weeks in the best of weather, and a safe journey was far from certain. Some ships never reached port, lost to storms or pirates. Illness inevitably spread through the cramped and unsanitary passenger quarters below deck. But John had more worries than just surviving the trans-Atlantic voyage. He was a young man in his twenties, and already John was a penniless failure, his life seemingly ruined. Now he was returning home, to his parents and brothers and sisters at their farm in Salem Village, Massachusetts (today's Danvers), where he surely faced the anger and disappointment of his father, John Porter Sr.

The two had last seen each other in happier circumstances, some months or years before, when John had set off to see the world and try his hand at business. The elder Porter provided funds and trade goods—the enormous

The John Porter house in Old Salem Village, Massachusetts.

sum of about four hundred pounds, for two voyages to Barbados and a third to England—with disastrous results. Somehow John lost all the money, and, even worse, he wound up in a London debtors' prison. Bailed out by his father's friends and put on a ship headed for Boston, John had little reason to expect a warm welcome from his family. But the pious John Sr., a devout member of Salem's Puritan community, apparently tried to draw inspiration from the biblical story of the prodigal son. As others later described the reception the Porters gave young John upon his return, "His parents entertained him with love and tenderness as their eldest son, and provided for him [what] was expedient and necessary."

That last phrase hints at punitive measures inconsistent with the "love and tenderness" that the Porters evidently tried to feel for their wayward son. And the elder Porter, despite his efforts to forgive John's "prodigal waste" and "riotous" expenditure of money, remained bitter. When John Sr. took sick in 1657 and believed himself near death, he made a will that barely provided anything for John Jr.—just a horse, five pounds in cash, and half an acre of land—a seemingly stingy bequest from such a prosperous father. John Sr. did not die, after all, and when he recovered, his friends "told him that he had done wrong in giving his son so little."

Undoubtedly his son learned about the provisions of the will, which laid bare the father's resentment and the young man's tenuous financial prospects. John Jr., as the eldest son of an affluent middle-class farmer, had learned no particular trade, had no money or home of his own, and had never married—and now he had little hope of gaining these essential elements of an independent life. He had failed at the one chance his father had given him to make his fortune. John's father could not forgive him, and perhaps John could not forgive himself.

From that point on, family relations at the Porter household deteriorated—sharply, shockingly. Maybe the father's animosity grew more open, or the son's desperation and self-loathing became unbearable, but whatever the reason, John Jr. exploded with rage. He no longer could control his tongue, and words poured forth—"profane, unnatural and abusive"—toward his father and mother. He called his parents "hypocrites," and John Sr. was so offended by this disrespect that he decided in 1661 to have his son arrested. The father obtained a warrant from the Essex County Court and delivered it personally to his son, who reacted by tearing up the paper and "uttering words in contempt of authority." Calling the judges by "vile names," young John declared, "I will not go before them: I will go before better men than they be."

Predictably, John Jr. ended up in Salem's house of correction to await trial. The stakes were high, for it was a capital offense under Massachusetts law to rebel against one's parents:

> *If a man have a stubborn or REBELLIOUS SON, of sufficient*
> *years & understanding (viz) sixteen years of age, which will*
> *not obey the voice of his Father, or the voice of his Mother,*
> *and that when they have chastened him will not harken unto*
> *them: then shall his Father & Mother being his natural par-*
> *ents, lay hold on him, & bring him to the Magistrates assem-*
> *bled in Court & testify unto them, that their Son is stubborn*

> *& rebellious & will not obey their voice and chastisement, but lives in sundry notorious crimes, such a son shall be put to death.*

No one had ever been executed in the Bay Colony for this crime, but young Porter surely realized that he was in danger.

From jail John sent his father a long, apologetic letter, lamenting the "doleful falling out between your self and me" and begging his family's forgiveness, claiming "with . . . real humility and unfeigned submission, I desire from my soul to make my peace with you." Although John was, by then, nearly thirty years old, he promised, "in the word of a true child," to behave in the future to "merit your and my mother's love, [or] at least not incur your displeasure." John sent a similar petition to court, apparently convincing the judges of his sincerity. They fined him for "profane swearing" but released him from jail, back into his parents' custody, giving John another chance. Perhaps John and his family tried to make new start, but peace did not last long.

Two years later John's parents returned to Essex County Court with near-hysterical complaints about their son's "abhorred and unheard of rebellious opprobrious vilifying and threatening speeches and carriages against his natural parents putting them into frights and his father in fear of his life." These reports so alarmed the judges that they seized John, jailed him in Boston, and sent his case to the Court of Assistants for trial. This time the high court would decide whether John's rebellion was a capital crime.

The evidence, as before, centered mostly on John's words. According to witnesses, the young Porter accused his father of being a "thief, liar, and simple ape," and more crudely a "shittabed." He spoke of his mother in vulgar terms, calling her "Gamar [Grandma] Shithouse," "Gamar Pissehouse," and "the rankest sow in town." John's rantings were not limited to his family; he also "reviled Mr. Hathorne, one of the magistrates, calling him [a] base, corrupt fellow, and said he cared not a turd for him." And John's behavior had escalated beyond mere words, perhaps fueled by alcohol. Witnesses claimed that John was a drunkard, who took an axe and chopped down fences on the family farm, beat servants, and even attempted to stab his younger brother. Given an opportunity to testify, John "impudently denied some things, others he excused by vain pretences, and some he owned, but gave no sign of true repentance."

John's father could bear no more; he wanted his son executed! John's mother, however, refused to join her husband in demanding justice, and her "tender and motherly affections" saved her eldest son. The Court of Assistants sentenced Porter to a mock hanging—to stand at the gallows, rope around his neck, for one hour—to be followed by severe whipping (thirty-nine stripes), a heavy fine (two hundred pounds, which John surely had no means to pay), and further imprisonment with hard labor for an indefinite term.

Before punishment could be administered, John somehow escaped from his prison cell and fled to Rhode Island. But even a tolerant colony like Rhode Island (with no capital laws against rebellious sons) was unlikely to welcome a young man convicted of abusing his parents. Someone influential must have befriended John in exile, for he soon found help of the highest order there—from the king's royal commissioners, who happened to be in Warwick. The commissioners took the extraordinary step of agreeing to hear an appeal of John's case and to put him under "his majesty's royal protection" until the matter could be resolved. They returned with John to Boston in 1665, promising him freedom from "all molestation or restraint" while they conferred with Massachusetts authorities.

The Massachusetts General Court, which doubled as the colony's legislature and highest court of appeals, reacted with indignation when the commissioners delivered a letter announcing their review of the Porter case. The court appointed a committee of eight men (including Governor Bradstreet and Deputy Governor Danforth—whom we have met before and will meet again) to deal with the king's four agents, and a lengthy account of these negotiations is preserved in the colonial records. From the Massachusetts perspective, it was inexplicable that royal commissioners should seek to intervene on behalf of John Porter Jr., "the vilest of malefactors," a man deserving of capital punishment rather than royal protection. But what rankled the Massachusetts committee most was this unprecedented royal interference with colonial justice. If anyone could take appeals directly to the king, no colonial court decision could ever be deemed final, which would weaken "the hands of lawful [Massachusetts] authority."

Whether the king's commissioners reached a final decision on the Porter case is unclear. John returned to the Porter farm in Salem Village, but apparently neither he nor his family could find a way to live together in peace. Soon the Essex County Court was hearing from the Porters again. For example, a servant of the Porter family complained in 1668: "John Porter my masters son, being come home to his father and dwelling in the house is very often greatly disturbing the family. . . . I can have little rest or quiet for him almost daily abusing me by . . . slanderous reproachful words, miscalling of me . . . and threatening of me that I go in fear of my life. . . . I do not question but my master would relieve [me] if he knew how." Judges ordered John Jr. to be imprisoned, yet again (the jail term was not specified in the court records), but father and son were back home together, arguing as usual, by 1670. This time they agreed to have their differences arbitrated out of court—apparently, John Jr. wanted a piece of land called Skelton's Neck—but the arbitrators ruled that John Sr. should keep the land and pay his son 150 pounds. John Jr., who refused to take the money, turned to vandalism—tearing up fences on his father's property, cutting down trees, starting fires—his behavior increasingly out of control.

Finally, in 1676 the death of John Porter Sr. (at the age of eighty-one years) brought the feud to an end. There is no evidence that father and son ever reconciled. John Porter Jr. lived on for eight more years, dying in 1684 with few possessions and no house or land of his own. His remaining family members, and the Salem community, probably felt little but relief at his passing. And perhaps the Massachusetts legal authorities learned something from this long-running family tragedy, for never again did any "rebellious son" face the gallows for disobeying his parents.

DANCING IN THE "NIGHT SEASON"

The word *Puritan* conjures up dour images of seventeenth-century New Englanders: praying in a cold, gloomy meetinghouse, reading the Bible by candlelight, wearing drab clothing and broad-brimmed hats, sitting in the stocks for punishment. We rarely think of Puritans as people who had fun. But human nature was not so different three hundred fifty years ago. Puritans—particularly teenagers and young adults—enjoyed hanging out with their friends and attending parties, just as their twenty-first-century counterparts do today.

Drinking alcohol was not prohibited at gatherings in colonial New England (beer and cider were common daily beverages for all members of the family), although drunkenness was a punishable offense. Secular music was not forbidden at parties, and many Puritans at all levels of the social hierarchy owned and played musical instruments. Even dancing was generally legal, except at weddings and taverns in Massachusetts, where authorities feared that disorderly conduct might result.

Puritans nonetheless kept close watch on youthful merrymaking, particularly when it involved unmarried men and women. For example, court records tell of a "lascivious meeting" one fall evening in 1660, after militia training practice in Cambridge, Massachusetts. A group of men (including Harvard students) and their young women friends (some who were visiting from Watertown, across the river) drank wine together at Andrew Belcher's ordinary, or tavern, the Blue Anchor, on Brighton Street. The party moved on, probably when the tavern closed at the usual 10:00 P.M. curfew time, up the street to Harvard Yard and into student rooms at the new brick dormitory called the Indian College. Witnesses saw a couple holding hands, a girl sitting on a boy's lap, and other amorous behavior that shocked the sensibilities of proper Puritan judges, who admonished the participants to "avoid the like loose practices for the future."

But no amount of judicial rebuke could curb Puritan partying, and young people continued to meet (often in secret) for fun and romance. One early Cambridge court file—a sheaf of fragile, ink-splotched papers now preserved at the Harvard University Archives—recounts a series of furtive parties over a two-week period beginning in December 1676, as New England was recovering from the devastations of King Philip's War. The General Court had just ordered a "day of humiliation"—a somber time of prayer and meditation—but many Cambridge residents simply wanted to relax and be happy again. Puritans did not celebrate Christmas or ring in the new year, but as soldiers returned from war and friends reunited, they arranged parties, in private homes and at Harvard College. These postwar gatherings seem tame and innocent by modern standards, but someone decided to report the partygoers to authorities. The informant, perhaps motivated by a straitlaced moral code or resentment at being excluded from the festivities, knocked on the door of a Cambridge magistrate, Thomas Danforth (who also appears in chapters 1, 2, 6, and 10, as well as earlier in this chapter).

Danforth launched an immediate investigation—some might call it an inquisition—with a prosecutorial fervor seemingly disproportionate to any possible offense. Perhaps he still grieved the wartime loss of his own son, killed battling Indians almost exactly one year before at the age of twenty-one. Many people believed that the death and destruction suffered in King Philip's War was God's punishment for colonial sins, so maybe Danforth feared God's wrath if he did not take stringent measures against the slightest hint of youthful immorality. The Massachusetts General Court, on which Danforth served, had recently tried to regain heavenly favor by clamping down on all manner of excesses—from men's long hair to "vain fashions," rudeness, idleness, and other "loose and sinful customs." Danforth could not afford to be lenient, not when the very safety of New England might be at stake.

The magistrate started questioning college men first on January 4, 1677, probably at his home just north of Harvard Yard. James Allin, a seventeen-year-old freshman from New Haven, Connecticut, confessed that a non-student friend (intriguingly named Onesephorus Stanley) stopped by his chambers on the morning of December 29. Allin had hard "cider fetch[ed] in," and they drank at least three quarts over a period of several hours, while other students "were coming and going." The next witness, another Connecticut freshman, was Thomas Barnard, who admitted "occasionally going into Allin's chamber" that day. He also revealed details of a party there on January 3, when Barnard found Stanley and some Harvard students in Allin's room again, drinking rum. They sent Barnard out to buy another pint, "which was mixt with water and sugar," and they "drank it among them but he saw no excess." One more student testified, a Harvard upperclassman and monitor, Thomas Cheever, who made it clear that he was above all this alcoholic frivolity—literally, for he lived in the room above Allin's. Cheever did not go downstairs to check what was happening, but he *heard* people "drinking and carousing," as well as the "voice of Onosephorus Stanley, . . . swear[ing] sundry times."

Danforth managed to track down Stanley (who seems to have had no permanent residence or family), and the magistrate learned that the nineteen-year-old was a frequent visitor to Harvard, sometimes staying overnight there with friends. Under Danforth's persistent questioning, Stanley disclosed the names of two other "drinking and carousing" students: Urian and Laurence Oakes, sons of the Harvard College president! At this point, Danforth seems to have dropped the Harvard investigation—questioning the president's sons could be politically sensitive—but Stanley's testimony offered even more surprises. Stanley revealed the identity of an older, nonstudent drinking partner who joined them: Daniel Warro, a free African American in his early thirties, who had once been a slave to Danforth's friend and fellow Cambridge magistrate, Daniel Gookin. Like Stanley, Warro seems to have had no settled home address, but Danforth located the former slave and questioned him, too. Both Stanley and Warro turned out to be popular Cambridge party guests.

The scope of the investigation expanded beyond Harvard Yard, as Danforth summoned nearly twenty other men and women—mostly Cambridge residents and their servants, and a slave from a neighboring town—for a marathon of interrogations. At least one witness, twenty-four-year-old John Watson, actually had the audacity to tell Danforth, "I refuse to answer." But most of the others confessed, in detail. Danforth uncovered evidence of several unchaperoned gatherings at private homes, from late December to January 3—where unmarried men consorted with single women, and people of different races and social classes partied together as equals.

One of the first December parties was a nighttime rendezvous at the home of the Cambridge blacksmith Abraham Arrington (spelled variously Errington, Erinton, Herrington and Harrington), who lived on the eastern side of Brighton Street (today's JFK Street, about midway between Harvard Square and Mt. Auburn Street). While Abraham and his wife supposedly slumbered in bed, their daughters—sixteen-year-old Mary and twenty-year-old Hannah—entertained several young men and women friends who ranged in age from their teens to early thirties (Daniel Warro was the oldest). The guests brought rum and cider to drink, and the party went on from about 9:00 P.M. to 2:00 A.M., until the noise purportedly woke Abraham Arrington and "he called to them to be gone."

A few days later, the brothers Ephraim and Thomas Frost (both in their midtwenties) invited people to their house north of Harvard Square (daringly close to Thomas Danforth's residence). They served rum and cider in the "night season," and the guest list was surprisingly diverse—some of the same group who attended the Arrington party, including the blacksmith's daughters, men and women servants, Daniel Warro—and even an African slave, Daniel's brother Silvanus (whom we will hear from again, in chapter 5). Although Silvanus lived more than five miles away, with the Wade family of Medford, somehow he slipped off that December night with another servant, Peter Hay, to attend the party. Danforth apparently managed to question the slave, who admitted that he had "liquor and cider to drink" and that he and his brother "did daunce and some of ye company sing" until after midnight.

Late-night singing and dancing could hardly go unnoticed in a small town like Cambridge, but when no constables or angry neighbors burst in to break up these gatherings, the partygoers perhaps believed that they could make more open arrangements. Hannah Arrington and her married friend Deborah Cane decided to host a bring-your-own-bottle supper and dance party on January 3. They planned the menu (roasted pork, turnips, apple pie, and coffee), cooked all day at the Cane house on Brighton Street, and hosted a large group, including Onesephorus Stanley and Daniel Warro, who showed up after the town curfew with rum and other liquor for a long night of feasting, drinking, singing, and dancing. Maybe the Cane party was bigger or louder than the others, for the next day word reached Thomas Danforth. His investigation put a stop to the round of winter merrymaking.

Over the next several days, Danforth penned pages of notes and confessions. When he had collected enough evidence, he sent Andrew Bordman, a constable, to apprehend most of the witnesses again, and at 10:00 A.M. on January 9, 1677, Danforth convened a special court session at the Cambridge ordinary, probably Andrew Belcher's Blue Anchor tavern. There, in the best parlor, Danforth called each of the accused before him, one by one. Presumably they had a chance to speak before Danforth pronounced judgment.

The lightest punishment went to a long list of partygoers—John Mirrick, Mathew Abdore, Ephraim Philips, Kt. Mudgin, John Collar, David Alexander, "Scilvanus Negro," William Cutter, John Dixon, Hannah Arrington, Mary Arrington, Mary Ruggles, and Ellinor Bowker—who were fined for

Deposition of "Silvanus Negro," January 8, 1676.

"being . . . out of ye house of their Parents and meeting at unseasonable times, and of night walking, and companying together contrary to civility."

Danforth singled out the wandering party guests Onesephorus Stanley and Daniel Warro for more severe treatment. Stanley was convicted of multiple offenses: "frequenting ye college and drawing ye students from their studies, . . . procuring Rum . . . to be . . . drunk in their chambers," "living from under family governance," and "being a night walker . . . of . . . dissolute behaviour." Not only was Stanley ordered to pay a large fine, but he also was given one month to "procure himself a master," or a settled household in which to live, "on penalty of being committed to Brideswell," the Cambridge prison. Daniel Warro, similarly "convicted of being a common night walker, and of refusing to submit to family order and governance," was sentenced "to be openly whipt 15 stripes."

Adults who had allowed their houses to be used for parties—Abraham Arrington, the Frost brothers, and Jonathan Cane (Deborah Cane's husband)—received heavy fines, having been convicted of "entertaining sundry young persons of both sexes, other men's children and servants, unseasonably in ye nighttime contrary to law." But Arrington, whose daughters Mary and Hannah attended the parties, was guilty of an even more serious offense: daring to criticize—perhaps even to mock—judge Thomas Danforth. Witnesses reported that the Cambridge blacksmith spoke openly to people at Andrew Bordman's shop down the street, just before the court session, expressing "much dissatisfaction" with Danforth's investigation and "saying it was a sad thing young persons could not meet together"—that "a young man and a maid could not be together"—without causing authorities to overreact. An outraged Thomas Danforth convicted Abraham Arrington "of uttering seditious and naughty words."

None of the Harvard College students received punishment (not publicly, at least). Perhaps Danforth kept that investigation under wraps, to avoid embarrassing the Harvard president and his sons. If James Allin and his friends continued surreptitious partying, their social life did not seem to affect their academic achievement. In fact, a few months later, Harvard awarded James Allin the honorific title "Scholar of the house." In 1679 Allin graduated third in his class, and Thomas Barnard graduated fourth. Both went on to serve as New England ministers, probably preaching against the evils of "drinking and carousing" in the "night season."

Chapter 4

TAVERN TALES

Despite its reputation for dour piety, Puritan New England did not ban alcohol. As we have seen, beer and hard cider were common daily beverages, and colonists indulged in "strong waters" of other sorts. Almost every town licensed one or more ordinaries, or taverns, ostensibly for the convenience of travelers and strangers, but local patrons also made frequent use of these facilities, to unwind after a hard day's work and catch up with friends on news and gossip.

Not surprisingly, in seventeenth-century New England many cases of lawbreaking and misbehavior involved alcohol or taverns, or both. The first story in this chapter, "Drinking with the Drummer," describes the near-riotous results when a New Haven man ventures into the bartending business. Then, in "Cider and Cakes for Highwaymen," three young men plot a crime spree at their local tavern and are scarcely out the door when they put their plans into action.

DRINKING WITH THE DRUMMER

Robert the Drummer stood in the market square of 1640s New Haven every morning, waking the town with a thumping reveille. Regardless of weather, residents expected this wake-up call (even if they might not have appreciated it), for the Puritans were industrious people, accustomed to rising before sunup and working hard all day. Few colonists owned clocks or pocket watches, so the night watchman woke the town drummer, Robert Bassett, when the morning sky began to lighten, and Robert made sure that the rest of New Haven did not oversleep or miss important events. He drummed to assemble the populace for Sabbath meeting; he drummed to summon the militia on training day; he drummed to herald the start of a court session; he drummed for emergencies, when ships arrived in the harbor, and on many other occasions.

All of that drumming required time and energy but did not bring Robert much money—four pounds was the annual salary funded from town coffers—and Robert had a young family to support and a mortgage to pay on his house "by the creek." When not drumming, Robert (like most other men in the colony) was a planter, with land to cultivate and crops to harvest, but he supplemented his income by making shoes, working at the shipyard, and taking whatever jobs he could find. Late one summer evening, someone convinced him to make money yet another way—by selling sack.

Sack was the seventeenth-century name for Spanish or Portuguese wine, similar to today's sherry, and the strongest (and most popular) sack came from the Canary Islands or Malaga, Spain. New Haven, as a busy port town, had access to imported sack and other wines and liquors, which people could drink at their local tavern. Robert did not have a tavern license, but somehow, in 1648, he acquired a large quantity of sack; perhaps he traded liquor and other goods on the wholesale market, or maybe he simply liked sack and kept it at home for personal use. His friends from the shipyard, apparently aware of Robert's inventory, knew where to go on a Friday night in July, when they met up with some other thirsty sailors just after sundown. Ten men showed up at Robert's house: a local man named Thomas Toby, four shipbuilders, crew from the ship *Susan* (including a mariner, Charles Higginson, and a boatswain named Badger), and the captain "of a pinnace [a light sailing ship] lately come in from Boston." They opened Robert's door "and called for sack."

Robert evidently tried to obey the letter of the law. He told the men that he had no license to serve liquor in "small quantities" by retail. But the sight of ten men at his doorstep, all ready to pay cash for alcohol, encouraged Robert to think creatively. Although the law prohibited dispensing small quantities without a license, Robert knew of no rules regulating the retail sale of liquor in *large* quantities. Therefore, Robert convinced himself that nothing would be wrong with selling sack to the seamen, and letting them drink it in his house, as long as they bought *enough* of it. Three quarts, Robert decided, was a large enough amount. So he informed the would-be customers that he could "not draw less than three quarts" at a time from the casks of sack in his cellar. The men happily paid, and drank, and when they wanted more, Robert continued to provide sack in three-quart amounts.

Three quarts multiplied several times meant gallons of sack, shared by the ten seamen. (Robert probably drank some too, to be sociable.) Before long, the men were "in their cups" and quarreling. The pinnace captain insulted Badger the boatswain, calling him "Brother Loggerhead," and Badger challenged the captain to go outside and fight. They fell "first to wrestling, then to blows," but soon the struggle grew so fierce that the captain feared "the boatswain would have pulled out his eyes, and the marks of the blows appeared some days after upon his face. . . . In this rage and distemper they tumbled on the ground, down the hill into the creek and mire, shamefully wallowing" there. Charles Higginson of the *Susan* jumped into the fray, "siding with the boatswain," and the outnumbered captain, thinking that he was about to be murdered, broke away and yelled for help, running "about the street crying, 'Ho, the watch! Ho, the watch!' " All this noise alerted the night watchman, who rushed to the rescue. As the watchman held off the drunken *Susan* sailors, the pinnace captain stumbled back to shore for a hasty retreat, while Badger "fell a swearing . . . as if he were not only angry with men, but would provoke the high and blessed God."

When the captain arrived at "the water side," however, he discovered that the tides were not cooperating with his escape to the anchored pinnace offshore ("the season not serving to go on board," as the court records described the situation). Too inebriated to think of anything else to do, the captain "returned to Robert Bassett's house, and there the boatswain fell upon him again." This time, instead of brawling in the street, the two men thrashed about and tried to kill each other *inside* the house, as Robert's wife and child screamed in terror. Robert, of course, had to do something to protect his family and to end this failed experiment in bartending. He "thrust the owner of the pinnace out of doors," threatening to "beat out his teeth" and "make him suck as long as he lived."

By now, although it was late at night and long past curfew, a crowd was gathering outside Robert's house. "The disorder was very great and very offensive, both to ye neighbors" and to others in the town, since "the noise and oaths [could be] heard to the other side of the creek." Somehow, in the confusion, the captain ran off again and managed, on this second try, to reach his ship and leave the harbor. Robert, Higginson and Badger, however—who looked more intoxicated and battered than the other sack drinkers—were arrested and thrown into jail. New Haven residents, their Friday night sleep already interrupted, may have been grateful that the imprisoned Robert could not wake them with his usual drumming early the next morning.

A few days later, released on bail, Robert—with Higginson, Badger, Toby, and the four shipbuilders—appeared in court to answer for their "several miscarriages, to the great provocation of God, [and] the disturbance of ye peace." Robert, an honest man, denied nothing about the wild night of drinking and fighting; in fact, he confessed (and we can almost imagine Robert smiling wryly as he said this) that "he had not seen the like since he came [to New Haven]." But the judges were not amused. First, they scoffed at Robert's peculiar idea that he could legally sell *large* (but not small) quantities of liquor at his house without a license—"a most perverse interpretation and abuse of" the law, they said, "as if the court would further drunkenness, forcing men to drink more then they desired." Surely Robert should have known better, the judges decided, and they found him guilty—not only of allowing men "to come in, spend their money and sit drinking at such unseasonable hours," but also of "quarreling and threatening, with the spirit . . . of a man distempered with rage or drink." His punishment was a hefty five-pound fine.

The other men got off with comparatively light sanctions. Badger, boatswain of the *Susan,* was convicted of "distemper in drinking, . . . quarreling, fighting, and swearing," but he brought two witnesses who persuaded the court that his behavior had been "fair and free from swearing" until that fateful night at Robert Bassett's house. That testimony "did mitigate the censure," the judges concluded, but they nonetheless fined Badger forty shillings, and his *Susan* crew member Charles Higginson ten shillings. Although Thomas Toby denied being "distempered in drink," his fine was five shillings, because "he had a share in the disorderly drinking" and helped Robert to dispense the sack. As for the four shipbuilders, no one could prove "excess in drinking, quarreling, or any other miscarriage, save their being in company in this disorderly meeting," so the court merely "advised them to take it as a warning" for the future. The pinnace captain from Boston (who sailed beyond the court's jurisdiction, perhaps with a mouthful of broken teeth) never appeared in court.

From Robert's perspective, his five-pound fine—more money than he earned all year as town drummer—probably seemed excessive punishment for someone who merely made a mistake about the liquor laws and then tried to restore order when other people misbehaved. He refused to pay the fine and demanded that the judges reconsider, but they were unsympathetic. Robert tried to raise more money at "ship work," but that kept him so busy in the fall of 1648 that he forgot to beat the drum for training day—with the result that the militia failed to show up. Robert remembered to drum the next time judges convened in New Haven, but he went home after the drumming and lingered so long over breakfast that he was late to court (where the local sergeant was complaining about Robert's training-day neglect). When Robert finally arrived in court, he argued and made excuses, and although the judges seemed annoyed, they decided to "pass it by for this time, without a fine."

The next summer, in 1649, Robert notified New Haven officials of his serious financial problems, owing to "some loss he hath had," and his "doubts [about] whether he shall ever be able to pay" off the loan for his house. Perhaps that five-pound fine threw Robert too far into debt, or he was simply growing weary of drumming and disgruntled with life in New Haven. Whatever the reason, Robert soon left New Haven, resettling his family forty miles down the coast at the new town of Stamford. But the long arm of New Haven authority reached even there, for New Haven claimed jurisdiction over Stamford. Robert became a leading spokesman for Stamford settlers, protesting New Haven rule, and he openly declared that "we can have no justice" from the New Haven courts. He ended up a prisoner for fomenting rebellion (a story worthy of its own chapter in some future book), and he was appointed chief drummer for a Stamford military expedition against the Dutch—a fight that never occurred. Maybe life still was not exciting enough for Robert after that, or he wanted (like the pinnace captain) to move beyond New Haven's jurisdiction. In 1654 he sailed his family across Long Island Sound, to try his luck in the New York Colony.

CIDER AND CAKES FOR HIGHWAYMEN

Long before the witch trials of 1692, John Higginson, a minister, worried about evils lurking in Salem, Massachusetts. In 1678 he sent a sharply worded petition to the Essex County Court, but it was not witchcraft that prompted Higginson to speak out. Instead, Higginson warned of another serious danger: the "sin of drunkenness and the excessive number of drinking houses" in town. He pointed out that Salem possessed an astounding number of "ordinaries and public drinking houses"—and he listed them all, a total of fourteen, licensed and unlicensed, and at least four more new taverns seeking liquor licenses. On behalf of the good "church members, freemen and sober people of Salem," Higginson beseeched the court to destroy "all such public houses . . . not . . . absolutely necessary for the entertainment of travelers and strangers."

Although drunkenness occurred throughout colonial New England, Salem seemed to have a particular penchant for alcohol. Perhaps Salem's maritime culture contributed to the proliferation of taverns—to accommodate hard-drinking sailors who came ashore with time and money on their hands—but transient seamen were not the only people who drank too much. Local farmers, laborers, and businessmen—and sometimes even their wives—frequented Salem's seventeenth-century taverns, and the court records paint a picture of boozy, smoke-filled rooms and disorderly behavior.

In February 1678, for example, only a few months before Higginson's complaint about the "sin of drunkenness," the Salem Commissioners Court heard testimony about a brawl at the home of John and Hanna Mason, who apparently kept an unlicensed tavern. Richard West happened to be walking by the house when he heard someone cry out: "The rogue will kill me!" West rushed inside and saw John Mackene fending off blows from Peter

Joy, while Humphrey Williams and Goody Mason looked on, all of them clearly inebriated. Two other Salem neighbors heard the uproar—Henry West, a tithingman, and Samuel Gardner, who was looking for his servant—and they also came in to find themselves in the middle of a drunken fracas. Goody Mason, apparently realizing that the tithingman would report them to the authorities, lunged for him with a heavy andiron, yelling, "Thou West, thou Harry, thou Devil," until someone seized the weapon from her hand. She then grabbed a chair to throw at Henry West, but she was too intoxicated and unsteady on her feet to stand, and she fell down. Gardner (who was a gentleman and could not be expected to deal personally with such rowdiness) urged West to do his duty as tithingman. West understandably feared bodily harm, and he sought help from Peter Joy, who had stopped fighting with Mackene and seemed the soberest, but Joy refused. Somehow the unfortunate West managed to enforce order, and Salem judges fined the drunken patrons. For her abusive words and attempts to strike the tithingman, Hanna Mason faced the choice of a fine or a whipping.

Although the Mason case may have helped to provoke John Higginson's anti-tavern petition, a shocking crime spree in late 1676 was certainly on his mind. For a few nights in December, three men on horseback terrorized Salem, robbing and assaulting people along the King's Highway. When the law finally caught up with the villains, they turned out to be young Salem residents—Thomas Leonard, Samuel Moore, and Blaze Vinton. Perhaps they fancied themselves to be romantic cavalier bandits, like the legendary highwaymen who stole from travelers in the English countryside. They may have needed money, particularly Leonard and Moore, who both had suffered recent legal problems and financial losses; Leonard was suspected of arson in the unexplained burning of a coal house at the Rowley Village ironworks, and Moore was fined for having sexual relations with his wife before their marriage. Whether Leonard, Moore, or Vinton was drunk when the trio ambushed their victims is hard to know. But shortly before the final attack, these would-be highwaymen fortified themselves with pots of hard cider and fresh-baked cakes at the Salem tavern owned by George Darling.

It was December 9, 1676, when Leonard, Moore, and Vinton left Darling's tavern, mounted their steeds, and rode off into the thickening dusk. They did not travel far, for just down the road, between Darling's and the next house, they heard the unmistakable sound of horses' hooves. The three high-waymen waited, silent, until the moment was right. Just as the shadowy fig-ures of approaching riders came into view, Leonard took the lead. He rode his horse into the center of the road, Moore and Vinton behind him, and shouted the age-old challenge: "Who goes there?"

Three other horsemen halted. "We are men!" was the reply, a boldly jovial, and perhaps foolhardy, response from a man named William Lattimore. A companion, John Trevitt, added, "We are friends." The travelers, journeying

from Boston, probably had no reason to expect trouble—highway robbery was uncommon in New England—so they spurred their horses to ride on by. But Leonard and his cohorts blocked the way.

"Dismount!" Leonard ordered. "We bid you stand."

The three victims—Lattimore, Trevitt, and Richard Simons—still could hardly believe what was happening, and they hesitated. The standoff contin-ued, and Leonard's tone grew nasty. Repeating his demand that the men get off their horses, he challenged Lattimore to prove his manhood and threat-ened, "I will take you by your eyelids and make your heels strike fire." The startled travelers now understood they were in danger, but it was too late.

Leonard and Moore plucked Lattimore off his horse and roughed him up until he handed over a gold ring, two shillings, some "gold ribbon and four yards of silver twist." Simons was carrying a large amount of money (one hundred pounds in cash), so he tried to escape, but the highwaymen soon overtook him, yanked him off his horse, and made chase when he fled on foot. They struck him "as many as a hundred blows," while Lattimore got back into the fight, crying, "Murder! Murder!" Blaze Vinton, who until then had been watching from the sidelines, realized that things were getting out of hand. He decided to intervene before someone actually got killed, attempting to pull his friends off Simons and Lattimore and stop the violence.

The commotion became loud enough for patrons at Darling's to hear. Several people raced outside to the rescue, getting close enough to recognize the attackers as the same young men who had had cider and cakes at the tavern earlier in the evening. In a panic, Leonard, Moore, and Vinton jumped back on their horses and rode away, but it was only a matter of time before constables tracked them down. The Salem highwaymen went on trial in March 1677 at Essex County Court in Ipswich.

Other victims came forward with their stories of December encounters with the three men. John Stacy told how they intercepted him in the fields south of Salem, snatched off his hat, and galloped away. Leonard Bellringer testified about a more serious incident one Saturday night, as he laid his "net lines" at the foot of the Forris River bridge (probably preparing a weir for fishing). Three horsemen came along—Bellringer now identified them as Leonard, Moore, and Vinton—and it was Samuel Moore who initiated the abuse. He leaned down from his horse, snagged the lines with a long stick, and threw them into the river, threatening Bellringer: "You dog! Fetch them out or else I will . . . throw you into the river." Bellringer had to wade into the river to retrieve his lines, and when he returned to shore, Moore and Leonard beat him. The highwaymen rode off with this parting advice: "Never sit on a bridge when gentlemen pass by."

But the three highwaymen were no gentlemen, by anyone's definition, and the Essex County Court concluded that they deserved severe punishment for the robberies, beatings, and other harassment. Instead of a whipping, which the young men probably expected, the judges ordered a more lasting, painful, and humiliating penalty—branding with a hot iron (the letter "B," perhaps for "bandit") on their foreheads. Before the sentence could be carried out, Blaze Vinton gained a last-minute reprieve from surprising sources. William Lattimore told the judges that he owed his life to Vinton, for pulling the other men off him; if not for Vinton, Lattimore said, he surely would have been murdered. And Bellringer made it clear that he had no complaint about Vinton, who did not participate in the assault by the bridge. Bellringer said of Vinton, "If I have but one shilling he shall have part of it, for when Moore and Leonard was foul on me, Vinton stood a pretty way from us and leaned on his horse and neither said nor did to my damage." The judges delayed the branding (apparently for all three men), but ordered them to post bonds for good behavior, to pay fines, and to return at the next court session. In June 1677 the court clerk penned this entry— "Blaze Vinton was cleared from his bond given for his good behavior"—and no further mention of the case appears in the court records.

Maybe Leonard and Moore reformed their ways, too, and the court quietly ignored the sentence of branding. A year later, when John Higginson went on his tirade against Salem's public houses, the judges responded with a polite order suggesting that only "the Ancientest, most suitable and most orderly houses and ordinary keepers" should have their licenses renewed. The court renewed George Darling's license in 1678 and for several subsequent years, so the crimes of his highwaymen patrons apparently were not held against him. Perhaps the three young men met again for innocent socializing—and cider and cakes—at Darling's tavern by the King's Highway.

Chapter 5

SLAVES AND SERVANTS

Although New England never developed the type of large-plantation economy characteristic of American colonies to the south, seventeenth-century settlers relied on labor from slaves and servants, even in the Massachusetts Bay Colony. People of color—Africans and Native Americans —were not the only people forced into involuntary servitude. The distinction between slave and servant was often blurred, especially in the 1600s, as the following stories demonstrate.

"The Irish Rebels" tells how two boys—kidnapped from their homes and shipped across the Atlantic for sale to a prominent English colonist in Massachusetts—finally staged their rebellion. And the second story, "Selling Silvanus Warro," is the poignant tale of an American-born African who never quite made his peace with the limitations of life in seventeenth-century New England.

THE IRISH REBELS

In May 1654 Captain George Dell sailed his ship *Goodfellow* into Boston Harbor, the last stop of a six-month voyage from England to Ireland to Virginia and finally to the Massachusetts Bay. Some Irish cargo, still unsold after trading in Virginia, remained below decks, and Dell was eager to dispose of that inventory. As Dell discovered when he disembarked and walked through Boston's crowded streets, he could not have arrived at a better time. The General Court was in session, gathering the colony's elected officials for biannual government business, and Boston teemed with out-of-town visitors. Dell would find plenty of customers, especially for the Irish servants that he was selling at bargain prices.

One of those buyers was the magistrate Samuel Symonds, who needed help on his Ipswich estate. Although Symonds rushed to the wharves as soon as he could take a break from his court duties, he apparently arrived too late for the best selection. By then, Captain Dell could offer only two young Irish boys—a child of about eleven years, Philip Welch, and an older youth named William Downing, who was disfigured by an unsightly skin condition. But Dell gave Symonds a good deal—no money down, and six months to pay in corn or cattle (hard currency being in short supply). And, although a typical indenture ran for five to seven years, these boys were so young that Dell added extra years to the terms, committing William to work for nine years and Philip for eleven, all for the low price of twenty-six pounds. Dell penned an official-looking bill of sale: "sould unto Mr Samuell two of the Irish youthes I brought over by order of the State of England."

After the General Court session ended, Symonds returned home to Ipswich with his new servants. The boys spoke little or no English, which made communication difficult. And William looked terrible (his body "ruffy" and "hassardous," as Symonds described the symptoms). A physician examined the boy and pronounced an alarming diagnosis—leprosy!—while a much-afflicted Mrs. Symonds "wept for fear of infecting the family." Fortunately, the doctor turned out to be wrong; maybe William suffered from scurvy or nutritional deficiencies after six months at sea, for his skin condition soon cleared up. William's health continued to be worrisome, however, and his work was interrupted on occasion by "a strong kind of fit" (epilepsy, perhaps), which could not be cured.

Even if the boys were not prime workers, Symonds considered himself lucky to acquire these Irish servants in the midst of a long-standing colonial labor shortage. Philip and William had no choice in the matter, and they learned to perform useful labor for the household. But as Philip grew into his teenage years, he began to rebel against the demands of his master and mistress. Since Symonds was a judge, he decided that some courtroom shock therapy might cure Philip's behavior problems. Hauling Philip into Essex County Court for "stubbornness and other offences," Symonds convicted his own servant and sentenced him to the house of correction. Then, probably assuming that the mere prospect of jail would cow Philip into submission, Symonds announced that the punishment would be "respitted until he again ha[d] cause to complain" about the boy. Hoping that he had put an end to Philip's stubborn ways, Symonds escorted his Irish worker back home.

But the courtroom incident failed to make Philip docile, and William, too, began to express discontent. Although six years had passed since Philip and William first came to Ipswich, still more years of servitude stretched ahead of them—five for Philip and three for William—a situation that they found increasingly intolerable. William dared to tell his mistress "that he would get free if he could, when he had served seven years," but Mrs. Symonds did not take him seriously. Penniless indentured servants, after all, had no power against a wealthy and important gentleman like Samuel Symonds. But Philip and William had more courage—and negotiating leverage—than anyone imagined. They chose a spring night, nearly seven years to the day after their sale at the Boston docks, to stage their revolt.

It was May 14, 1661, and the Symonds household (including Philip, William, a young servant named Naomi Hull, and family guests) gathered in the parlor, as usual, for prayers following the evening meal. Before Mr. Symonds could begin his Bible reading, Philip inquired about plans for the next day's work: "Is Goodman Bragg's son coming to plow?" Mrs. Symonds answered, "I think so," and then Philip asked, "Who will plow with him?" "One of you," she replied—meaning, of course, either Philip or William. Clearly, Mr. and Mrs. Symonds were unprepared for what would happen next.

Philip stood up (an unthinkable impertinence, as his master was about to pray) and made a dramatic announcement: "We will work . . . for you, no

Castle Hill farmhouse, built by John Winthrop Jr.,
was the home of the Samuel Symonds family in Ipswich, Massachusetts.

longer." Mr. and Mrs. Symonds stared, unsure whether this outburst was just a bad joke or a genuine rebellion. "Is it so?" Mr. Symonds asked. "What will you [do], play?" Philip persisted: "We have served you seven years. We think that is long enough."

Symonds tried to end this nonsense. "We must not be our own judges," he reminded his servants. "You must work for me still, unless you run away." William answered this time—"We scorn to run away"—but Philip explained that they were prepared to do so. "We will go away, and leave you before your faces. If you will free us, we will plant your corn, and mend your fences. If you will pay us as other men. But we will not," Philip emphasized, "work with you upon the same terms or conditions as before."

Perhaps Symonds hoped that the unexpected mutiny would blow over—it was plowing and planting season, the worst time for problems with his help—so he changed the subject. "Come, let us go to prayer." But the Irish servants would not be diverted. "You may go to prayer," Philip replied, as he and William headed for the door. "We will speak more in the morning." Symonds, however, would not negotiate. The next morning he summoned a constable to arrest and imprison his servants "for absolutely refusing to serve [their] master."

The case went to trial at county court in Salem, where Philip and William offered heartrending testimony. They were kidnapped from Ireland against their will, and no one ever consulted them about the terms of their sale. Other Irish witnesses corroborated this account, telling how English soldiers stole boys and men from their beds at night and brought them, weeping and grieving, to Captain Dell's ship *Goodfellow*. None of these Irish "servants" consented to be shipped across the Atlantic and sold to strangers. Despite their unwilling bondage, Philip and William told the jury that they gave Symonds the "best service" they could for "seven complete years," but they now wanted to be free.

The jury obviously sympathized, voting to release them from servitude, unless the contract between Dell and Symonds was legal. Only judges could decide that question of law—and Samuel Symonds was one of the four judges presiding at his own case. He showed his fellow judges the bill of sale (and its language about transporting "the Irish youths . . . by order of the

State of England"). He also pointed out that some servants "are bound to serve for near as long as these," and that living in New England offered poor Irish boys advantages they could never expect back home. But Symonds's best argument (calculated to worry judges who owned slaves or servants themselves under similar contracts) was that invalidating this sale could threaten "the Bargains of so many [others] in the Country." Not surprisingly, the "Court adjudged the covenant legal," ordering Philip and William to serve out their terms.

Five years later, apparently free at last, Philip Welch moved across the river to Wenham, where he married young Hanna Haggett. (William Downing, however, disappeared from the records, his fate unknown.) Philip and Hanna never prospered—they moved from town to town, "warned out" for their poverty—but the stubborn Irishman worked hard to build a new life in America for his family. And despite Philip's rebellious early years with Samuel Symonds, he evidently grew to respect his former master. In 1675, when a son was born to Philip and Hanna, they chose a surprising name: Samuel.

SELLING SILVANUS WARRO

In 1672 an African American named Silvanus Warro waited behind bars at Boston's town jail. He stood convicted of "stealing money from his master" and, even more serious, of fathering an Englishwoman's child. The Suffolk County Court imposed severe penalties. Warro's wounds had not yet healed from the whipping he received after the trial—"twenty stripes" on his bare back, which would leave him scarred for life. But corporal punishment was only part of Warro's sentence. The judges also ordered that he pay twenty pounds restitution for the theft and arrange for child support of "two shillings six pence per week"—impossible sums for a man in Warro's position unless his master or some other benefactor stepped forward to pay. The court, however, specified Warro's fate if he failed to raise the money: "The said Silvanus is to be sold."

Silvanus Warro had never before faced sale to a stranger. Born into slavery on a Maryland plantation in the early 1640s, Warro had belonged to the same owner—a Puritan named Daniel Gookin—for nearly thirty years. When Warro was still an infant, Gookin brought him to Massachusetts, where they lived with Gookin's wife and baby daughter in a Cambridge mansion house near Harvard College. Historical sources offer ample documentation of Gookin's life, for he became an active New England leader, serving as a judge on the Massachusetts Court of Assistants and as a commander of local militias. Gookin also devoted much energy to missionary work among the Native Americans, helping to establish "Praying Indian" towns for Christian converts. We would scarcely know about Gookin's slave Silvanus Warro, however, if the old court records had not survived to tell his story.

Little detail remains about Warro's childhood, except that he was "born bred and educated" in Gookin's household. Seventeenth-century slave owners often viewed African children as exotic pets—companions for their own sons and daughters—and Warro may have played that role in Gookin's family. Gookin admitted "natural affection" for the young slave and promised, in 1667, to set him free—but not right away. Perhaps Gookin wanted to provide Warro with further religious education in a godly Puritan household (Gookin himself was busy traveling throughout Indian country, instructing Native converts during those years)—or maybe Gookin simply needed additional cash—but whatever his reasons, Gookin delayed emancipation, hiring Warro out to work for Deacon William Park in Roxbury. Their agreement: if Warro gave Park eight years of faithful service, then Gookin would release Warro from slavery in 1675.

Life in Roxbury, however, did not work out as planned. Maybe Park was a harsh master, or Warro simply missed his lifelong home with the Gookin family, but in 1668 Warro rode a horse out of Park's stable and attempted, unsuccessfully, to escape. Park took Warro back, but before Warro could complete the requisite eight years of service, he got into trouble again. This time Warro became romantically involved with Elizabeth Parker, a young white servant in Park's home, and she found herself pregnant. Warro broke into Park's strongbox and stole money but the theft was discovered before they could flee. Elizabeth gave birth to a son, naming him Silvanus Warro Jr. Park evicted mother and baby, packing them off to Elizabeth's father in Lancaster, Massachusetts.

The elder Silvanus went to prison, unable to pay restitution for the theft or to support his child, and uncertain whether he would ever experience the

freedom that Gookin had promised. An unexpected jailhouse visit by
Gookin and Park may have raised Warro's hopes, but the Puritan gentlemen
offered no money, presenting him with two stark options: Gookin would
ship Warro to Virginia (for sale there), or Park would sell Warro to a local
slave owner, Jonathan Wade of Medford. Gookin advised Warro "to be content to live with Mr. Wade for else he must be sold out of the Country to
satisfy the Court's sentence." Warro undoubtedly preferred staying in
Massachusetts (with the chance of seeing Elizabeth and their son again), but
Gookin discouraged that interracial relationship, suggesting that Warro
instead "might fall in with Mr. Wade's Negro Wench and live well."

Warro left prison as the property of Jonathan Wade in 1672, while Elizabeth
struggled to care for Silvanus Jr. in Lancaster. Her father, Edmund Parker,
was a poor man living in a tumbledown shack of a home, but he welcomed
Elizabeth and her mulatto child. Lancaster selectmen, however, objected to
Elizabeth's "bastard" and tried to send the baby back to Roxbury. Parker
refused to surrender his grandson, and town officials pursued the matter in
court. Deacon Park, who held the proceeds of Silvanus's sale, apparently
sent none of it to Lancaster. Instead, Park proposed a solution that would
put even more money in his pocket: he would sell Silvanus Jr., too. The
court agreed, giving Park permission "to dispose of and put out to Service
the Child . . . till it be thirty years of age."

Although Edmund Parker continued to resist, Silvanus Jr. eventually was
"put out to Service," never receiving the financial support that his father's
sale was supposed to ensure. Warro remained in Medford with Wade, who
showed no intention of relinquishing him. Daniel Gookin, who tried to
maintain contact with Warro—even borrowing him on occasion from Wade
(see the illustration on page 58)—grew to regret his part in the unfortunate
situation, and he devised a plan to get Warro back.

On November 8, 1682, Warro made a furtive trip from Medford to
Gookin's house in Cambridge. There, as if he were free to contract for his
own labor, Warro signed an indenture agreement that Gookin had prepared:
"to serve and obey him . . . for the whole term of my natural life, he . . .
to provide me meat, drink, lodging and apparel . . . and so take care of me
in sickness and in health." When Wade realized that his slave was missing,
he sent constables on a hue and cry to find Warro—and to drag him back

Daniel Gookin's 1680 letter to Jonathan Wade: "I request you to give
your man Silvanus leave to come to my house . . . to helpe" at the wedding
of Gookin's daughter, "Silvanus being knowne to his old mistress to bee hand[y]."

to Medford. Prepared to fight for Warro in court, Gookin sued Wade for
"holding and detaining . . . his Servant Silvanus Warrow Negro." Gookin
presented a compelling case—questioning the validity of the 1672 court
order for Warro's sale, explaining how fifteen years of service for Park and
Wade had more than satisfied Warro's financial obligations, and asserting
that now, "if any have right to him tis myself who Bred him from a child."
Despite his well-reasoned arguments and impassioned pleas for justice,
Gookin lost the case. The court ruled that Warro was Wade's slave, and that
Wade could keep him for life.

Warro never gained his freedom, but his son finally returned to Boston in
1707, free after many years in servitude. Town selectmen feared that he
might be a financial burden and sent him away, penning this summary for
the official records: "Silvanus Warrow a Mollatto man being a Lame Cripple
. . . Says he formerly belonged to . . . Mr Budg of New Bristoll."
Traveling on to Medford, Silvanus Jr. was too late for a reunion—his father
by that time had died. He discovered, however, that he still had kin in servitude at the Wade household, a mulatto half-sister born from another interracial union of his father's. Silvanus Jr. vowed (and we do not know whether
he was successful) to "Git her free."

Chapter 6

NEIGHBOR VERSUS NEIGHBOR

When colonial New England neighbors squabbled, they often took their disputes to court. Anyone who thinks that the "litigation explosion" is a modern phenomenon has not read enough seventeenth-century court records! The following stories are only a small sampling of those cases, showing what happened when neighbors sued neighbors.

In "The Purloined Pigs," a determined Scotsman in Cambridge Farms, Massachusetts, wages a court battle against the aptly named Michael Bacon, for taking away his pigs. The second story, "Native Neighbors," tells how Indians of the Connecticut River Valley sought—and generally received—surprisingly even-handed justice from the Englishmen's courts. Finally, in "The Sudbury Standoff," a disagreement over the site for a new church erupts into violence and lays bare the hidden greed and prejudice in a quiet New England town.

THE PURLOINED PIGS

Anyone familiar with Lexington, Massachusetts, has seen the name Munroe—on signs for the historic Munroe Tavern, the Munroe Center for the Arts, and Munroe Road, to cite a few examples. The first Lexington Munroe, then spelled Munro or Munrow or sometimes just Row, was a Scotsman named William, who arrived at Boston Harbor with a shipload of other Scottish war prisoners in 1652. He worked as an indentured servant in Menotomy (today's Arlington), earned his freedom, and settled in Cambridge Farms, as Lexington then was known.

Most of what we know about William Munro—where he bought land and whom he married and when his children were born—tells us little about the kind of man he was. But a neglected source of information, old court records, still preserves stories from the lives of people like Munro, often in their own words. One such file from the Massachusetts Archives, *Row v. Bacon,* tells of Munro's stubborn quest for justice against an arrogant foe. I call this the Case of the Purloined Pigs.

The problems started on a Monday in late November 1671, after a heavy snowfall in a remote corner of Cambridge Farms, near today's intersection of Lowell and Woburn Streets. Here, at the house where Munro lived with his wife, Martha, and three small children, a neighbor arrived looking for his hogs.

Michael Bacon had a reputation for letting his hogs run wild, and this time they had wandered all the way from Bacon's house (in present-day Bedford, Massachusetts) to enjoy the companionship of Munro's pigs. Munro and his wife, wanting only to be rid of the uninvited swine guests, which were depleting their meager forage, helped Bacon to separate his hogs from their own. Bacon then headed off through the woods with his swine, and the Munros returned to their daily chores.

But Bacon's hogs apparently did not want to leave their friends, and they soon came back. This time, when Bacon returned to retrieve them, he did not bother to sort them out; he just drove the whole lot off, his *and* the Munro pigs. Seeing most of the family's worldly wealth hoofing away, Martha shouted at Bacon to stop, but he ignored her. William, who was occupied feeding the oxen or fetching firewood, had to drop everything, strap on snowshoes, and take off in pursuit.

Munro was not a man to be trifled with. He had endured many hardships—on the battlefield, in a prison camp, during the long Atlantic crossing and the years in servitude. Now he was free to farm his own little piece of land, and those pigs were crucial to his family's survival. Hogs meant meat on the table and income to buy other necessities of life, and Munro could not afford to lose a single animal.

He also knew that Michael Bacon could not be trusted. If the court records are any indication, Bacon was known throughout the county for making trouble. His hogs had damaged crops for miles around, but he always denied responsibility, blaming others for failing to keep their fences in repair or claiming that the hogs belonged to someone else. Bacon's name appears repeatedly in land disputes, cases of wandering horses and cattle, slander and forgery accusations, breach of contract, even a paternity case (as we saw in chapter 2). Thus, when Munro set off in the snow after Bacon and his pigs, he had good reason to expect problems.

Munro trudged north through three miles of drifted snow, following hog tracks until he finally overtook Bacon and found most of his livestock. One pregnant sow was "so tired and spent that she could not come back," and he had to leave her with Bacon. Another sow, also "big with pig," was missing. Munro was angry, but nothing more could be done before nightfall. He drove the rest of his hogs back home.

The next day Munro sought out John Gleison, a constable's deputy, and Gleison's brother, William. He showed them the hoof-trodden farmyard and the path through the woods, and together they trekked back to Bacon's house to retrieve the last two swine. Bacon's response was predictable. First he pretended the incident had never happened. Then, when the Gleisons clearly were not buying that story, he "confessed that William Row's swine was with him in the drift the day before, but . . . he did them no wrong," and he no longer had them "in his hands." "If Row lost them, he must go look for them." Bacon, of course, did not offer to help.

On Wednesday, the weary Munro turned to his neighbors John and Benjamin Russell, and together they scoured the woods for the missing pigs. They found one, stuck in a drift, amazingly still alive, and with "much difficulty" they got her home.

One sow was still missing, and Munro's patience was running out. He took the law-abiding next step, which required yet another long journey on foot through the snow. He walked to Cambridge, to the house of the magistrate Thomas Danforth (whose name is by now quite familiar) overlooking Harvard College, where he filed a claim against Bacon. Although this was a big deal to a farmer of Munro's modest means, the amount in controversy was small enough that the magistrate could resolve the dispute without resort to the courts. Danforth took up quill pen to issue a warrant, ordering Michael Bacon "to appear before me at my house, the last day of the week at 12 of the clock to answer the complaint of William Row, for violence done him in taking away his swine out of his yard, and driving them away."

At the appointed time, six people—William and Martha Munro, the Russells, and the Gleison brothers—crowded into the magistrate's study to testify. Danforth recorded the evidence with careful penmanship, and the witnesses all signed with their marks. Michael Bacon did not show up, and he lost the case. The constable's deputy set out to seize a branded steer from Bacon to ensure payment of Munro's damages.

Shortly thereafter, before Munro could collect a single shilling, his missing sow reappeared at his door. She was "lamed and went but upon three legs," delivered by a man who claimed that he "found" her and was asked by Bacon to take her home.

Bacon probably hoped that returning the sow would get him off the hook for damages, but Munro stood firm. In late December Bacon asked for a rehearing, which Danforth granted on January 29. The result was the same, only now Bacon owed more, a reflection of the added costs for witness time and constable's fees.

Still Bacon refused to pay, and he mounted a vigorous appeal, seeking a jury trial in the Middlesex County Court. He hired the Concord lawyer John Hoar (whom we will encounter again in chapter 10) to draft a tedious petition with a long series of technical arguments, from improper service of the attachment on his steer to misfeasance by the well-respected Danforth. The trial took place in Cambridge on April 2, 1672, probably at the local Blue Anchor Tavern. Someone apparently represented Munro at the trial (although his identity is not known), for an elegantly written legal argument appeared in the court records on Munro's behalf.

Complaint of "William Row and Martha his wife" against Michael Bacon.

The final result, after more than four months of legal wrangling, was judgment again in favor of Munro: "one pound sixteen shillings and four pence," plus court costs, a goodly sum, but probably less a financial boost than a moral victory for the dogged Scotsman. Presumably, Bacon paid up, for here the paper trail of *Row v. Bacon* ends. Munro returned to a quiet farming life, but Bacon continued to keep the courts busy in disputes with other neighbors.

NATIVE NEIGHBORS

On May 4, 1648, a Native American named Coe paddled his canoe across the Connecticut River from his village of Agawam to the town of Springfield, Massachusetts. Coe was angry. An Englishman, Francis Ball, had just beaten Coe's wife, and Ball's cattle were eating Coe's newly planted corn crop. Coe sought justice in the Englishman's court.

The magistrate William Pynchon penned an entry in his court diary: "Coe one of the Indians on the other side did complain against Francis Ball for striking of his wife two blows with a stick." Ball, when summoned to answer these charges, made light of the offense: "it was but two blows with a little short stick . . . not so big as his little finger and he struck her only on her bear skin coat." Pynchon ordered Ball to pay Coe's wife "2 hands of wampum" as recompense.

Ball protested the fine, arguing that Indian children "scared . . . and hindered his cattle" and thus provoked the conflict. In colonial New England, cattle and hogs foraged freely; farmers erected fences to protect their crops. If Ball's wandering livestock damaged Coe's corn, the fault was Coe's, for not fencing his cornfield. Evidently persuaded by Ball's reasoning, Pynchon fined Coe "3 hands" of wampum for the children's unlawful interference with English livestock, to be paid before Ball had any obligation to return "2 hands" for Coe's wife.

The Indian was no fool, and he reacted with disdain to a legal result leaving him worse off than if he had never ventured into the Englishman's court. He refused to exchange three hands of wampum for two, saying that he would give Ball "2 blows" instead. Coe, however, refrained from violence and managed to extract a valuable concession from Pynchon (which may have been Coe's objective in the first place; he probably used the complaint about his wife's beating as leverage). Pynchon granted Coe additional land to enlarge his cornfield, on the condition that "he would secure it against any cattle . . . or else if it were spoiled he would ask nothing for it." Coe returned to his village, no doubt considering his court trip a success.

Coe's case was not unusual. Many Native Americans went to court in seventeenth-century New England, and colonial judges administered surprisingly even-handed justice. The Pynchon diary paints a vivid picture of what happened in frontier Springfield, when colonists and their Native neighbors resolved their differences in court.

Shortly after Coe's case, an Indian with the intriguing name of Nippinsuite Jones sued another Springfield colonist for assault. This time, William Pynchon ordered severe punishment, sentencing Thomas Miller (whom we will meet again in chapter 8) to fifteen lashes for beating Nippinsuite "with the butt end of his gun." In 1659 Springfield livestock again ruined Indian cornfields. John Pynchon, who had succeeded his father as magistrate, sent appraisers to the site and ordered colonists "on that side of the River" to pay damages "according to the number of their cattle." Pynchon also proved sympathetic when an Indian complained of vandalism in 1664. As Pynchon's court diary described the case, "diverse young persons" snatched the Indian's birch-bark canoe from "Goodman Muns Garden" and took it to "the brook in the street, whereby the Canoe was made unserviceable." Since Pynchon was unable to identify the culprit who "broke or split the canoe," he ordered fifteen English youths to pay the Indian four pence each.

The May 1648 entry about Coe's case in William Pynchon's diary.

The Pynchon court also prosecuted Indians under colonial law. Intoxicated Indians, for example, faced the same ten-shilling fine imposed on drunken colonists. An Indian named Watsaw Luncksin was summoned to court in 1665, where he acknowledged a debt and confessed to "breaking the glass windows of Capt. Pynchon's farmhouse." In 1670 "Aquossowump alias Woquoheg" stole wampum from a chest in Samuel Bliss's house. The Bliss children, alone at home while their parents attended church, tried to prevent the theft by sitting "on top of the chest to keep it down," but the Indian overpowered them. John Pynchon sentenced Aquossowump "to be well whipped with 20 lashes" and "to pay his spare coat."

As a busy fur-trading hub, Springfield attracted Indians from faraway places, and they sometimes landed in court. Constables on horseback chased a band of Nipmucks after a scuffle at Thomas Miller's house, capturing three Indians and taking them back for trial. When a visiting New Haven Indian stole the "best red kersey petticoat and some linen in a Basket" from Thomas Rowland's house, however, the thief escaped, and Pynchon blamed neighboring Indians for thwarting his arrest. A local sachem paid Pynchon a visit, asking "to Speak with him in private" and offering "3 fathom" of wampum for court coffers, to make amends. After "some pause and conference together," they settled for five fathom (each fathom being a six-foot length of approximately 360 beads) and mutual promises that the English and Indians would live in peace.

All hope for peaceful coexistence ended, however, with King Philip's War. In 1675 Indian attacks devastated towns along the Connecticut River valley, and most of Springfield burned to the ground. After the war Springfield survivors rebuilt homes and barns, and John Pynchon continued to serve as the local magistrate, but he never again mentioned Indians in his court diary—except for one, an Indian named John Buck.

Pynchon's diary does not reveal John Buck's origins—whether Buck's family once lived in a neighboring Indian village, or whether the Indian arrived in Springfield long after King Philip's War. By the time that Buck showed up in Pynchon's diary, in 1690, he was a servant or slave, likely in Captain Samuel Glover's household. Buck was friendly with a Springfield colonist who may have worked for Glover too, John Crowfoote.

One July night Crowfoote and Buck shared a wooden quart bottle of rum; then, "in drink, if not drunk," they began wandering Springfield's streets at the unseasonable hour of 10 o'clock. They taunted the night watchmen, "reviling them and . . . roaring rudeness." Even worse, witnesses heard Buck "grievously swearing and profaning the name of God." The next day John Pynchon summoned both men to court and ordered ten lashes apiece, "well laid on upon the naked body." Buck received his whipping, but Captain Glover obtained Crowfoote's release by paying a fine instead.

After that incident, Crowfoote stayed out of trouble, marrying in 1692 and settling down. In November 1694, however, "John Buck the Indian" appeared again in John Pynchon's court. This time he was a fugitive slave, running from New York (where Glover apparently had sold him). The new master sent a hue and cry off to Springfield, suspecting that Buck might head for his old home, and authorities caught up with Buck near Crowfoote's house. Buck rode a stolen Springfield horse and carried provisions acquired in town—including a kettle belonging to John Pynchon, ten fowls, a loaf of bread, and even a "lace neck handkerchief."

Pynchon's diary recorded a plaintive interrogation, probing why Buck had fled his master, but Buck answered simply, "I know not for I cannot fault him." Clearly, no one wanted to punish Buck for the thefts—the victims refused to press charges—but Pynchon would not ignore the New York court order. We can only guess at Pynchon's thoughts as he penned his last court entry about this former Indian neighbor: "It now being Saturday night, I committed him to prison," and a deputy "undertook to carry him to New York to his master to whom he was accordingly delivered."

THE SUDBURY STANDOFF

The old First Parish Church in Wayland, Massachusetts, looks like the quintessential New England house of worship. On a sunny day the tall white steeple seems to glow, and light streams through the towering sanctuary windows to rows of pews inside. Set back on a slight rise above the intersection of Boston Post Road and Cochituate Road, the building appears ageless, an enduring haven in the midst of the modern world; and indeed, a church has occupied this site since the early 1800s.

Few people would ever guess, from looking at this peaceful setting, that the first effort to build a church here in 1724 nearly tore the town apart. Rival factions faced off at this spot with clubs and axes, one group determined to erect a new church, and the other just as resolute to prevent construction. At the heart of the standoff was a land dispute, fueled by neighborhood feuds and, perhaps, by lingering prejudice against one family whose origins in the community were different.

When the controversy erupted in the 1700s, this land (then part of the town of Sudbury) belonged to the Ross family. Their house stood just across the road, near the Mill Brook, where three generations of Rosses had lived for nearly sixty-five years. The first Ross in Sudbury was an accidental immigrant, a young Scotsman named James, who never intended to settle here. Pressed into service by his clan chief in the Scottish Highlands, James

First Parish Church, Wayland, Massachusetts, site of the eighteenth-century confrontation between James Ross Jr. and William Jennison.

fought for King Charles II in the English Civil War and was captured when Oliver Cromwell's troops defeated the royalist army in England at the Battle of Worcester. James and other Scots prisoners found themselves on a ship in 1651, exiled across the ocean to New England and sold into servitude. The English colonist who bought James was a Sudbury farmer, John Rudduck.

James, then only about sixteen years old, had a rocky start in the Sudbury community. From all accounts, Rudduck—a strong-willed young man who quarreled with his neighbors—could not have been an easy master. And James, a hardy Highlander and former soldier, was anything but subservient. Predictably, the two men clashed. In 1655 the Middlesex County Court convicted James "of shameful abuse and violence" toward his master and sentenced him to one of the most extreme corporal punishments found in the early Massachusetts records—"39 stripes." Two years later, still Ruddock's servant, James landed in trouble again. This time he was "convicted by his own confession of fornication . . . with Mary the daughter of Thomas Goodenow" (a neighbor and relative of John Rudduck). James was sentenced to another whipping—"twenty and one stripes on his naked body"—and the court ordered him to marry the young woman. Mary Goodenow, however, refused to marry the Scotsman, even though she had just given birth to a baby girl, choosing to be "whipped ten stripes" instead.

Later Mary had a change of heart. After James was released from servitude, she finally married him in December 1658, when their daughter, Mary, was about two years old. James rented a farm at first, and then, when Thomas Goodenow decided to relocate (joining Rudduck and some other Sudbury families at a new town named Marlborough to the west), James bought his father-in-law's Sudbury house and land. There James Ross stayed, with his wife and daughter and nine more children born over the next two decades. Those years were not trouble-free, marred by local tensions—the court ordered James to "keep the peace," for example, with his neighbor John Brigham—and James suffered property losses when Indians attacked Sudbury in 1676 during King Philip's War. But James managed to persevere and put down roots.

When James died in 1690, his son James Jr. took over the farm, supporting his mother and several sisters, and later a wife and children of his own. Although this second-generation Ross patriarch was not a rich man by any means, he probably assumed that his homestead was secure—as secure as it could be for any hardworking farmer who owned his house and fields and whose fortune depended on the richness of the soil and the vagaries of weather (and war). But there was a legal problem that James Jr. never suspected—a cloud on the title to his land.

The first hint of this problem did not come to light until 1709, when James Jr. was nearly fifty years old. He walked into the Ashen Swamp Meadow (one of Sudbury's common lands), chopped down an oak tree, and hitched up his oxen to haul the trunk back to his farm. To his surprise, a constable knocked on the door a few days later and delivered a court summons, suing James for trespass.

This lawsuit, instigated by a neighbor, William Jennison, and financed with town money, seemed incomprehensible to James Jr. at first. He—and his father before him, as well as other residents of the town—had cut wood and hay from Ashen Swamp Meadow over the years without incident. Use of the common lands was a right of all Sudbury landowners. And James Jr. could trace his ownership in an unbroken line from Sudbury's original settlers—from his grandfather Thomas Goodenow, who built the house and farmed this land, and his mother, Mary, who grew up here, to his father, James, who purchased the property in the early 1660s from Goodenow, before James Jr. was even born. But William Jennison and the Sudbury town selectmen had discovered a technical defect in the property title, which they seemed determined to exploit: when Thomas Goodenow sold this farm to his Scottish son-in-law, nearly five decades earlier, he neglected to record the deed. Without that official piece of paper on file with authorities, James Jr.'s rights to the Sudbury common lands—and to his own farm—were in peril. Were the Rosses little more than squatters on this Sudbury land?

James Jr. must have had sympathetic or influential friends, because the court records show that a prominent Boston attorney, Paul Dudley, successfully defended him in the Ashen Swamp Meadow lawsuit. And somehow, probably with Dudley's help, the Ross family's title to their Sudbury farm was secured in 1710 with the filing of proper legal paperwork. But the rift between James Ross Jr. and William Jennison never healed, and their enmity surfaced again in dramatic fashion a few years later, over the site for a new Sudbury church.

The town population had grown since the seventeenth century, as families expanded and Sudbury annexed land beyond its original territory, and by the early 1700s the western inhabitants had built their own church. Neither the western church nor the old east-side one, however, stood conveniently near William Jennison's land—he lived in the so-called Natick Farms, recently added to Sudbury's southern bounds—so Jennison began campaigning to move the east-side church closer to him. The perfect spot, Jennison decided, was on the Ross farm, in the field across from James Jr.'s house.

Not everyone agreed with Jennison, least of all the Ross family; in fact, Jennison's proposal threw the town into an uproar. Many residents saw no reason to move the east-side church after so many years, and certainly not closer to the "Natick farmers," who were relative newcomers. Some believed that Jennison was harassing the Rosses. Yet Jennison persisted, until a majority voted in favor of his plan at town meeting, and in 1723 the Massachusetts General Court authorized moving the Sudbury "Meeting House . . . about a mile South east from the place it now stands to the land of Mr. James Ross." Despite the General Court's approval, however, Sudbury could not just seize the Ross land for a church site; some legal niceties must be observed (especially since the Ross land title had been confirmed). But James Ross Jr. absolutely refused to sell.

Jennison would not take no for an answer, and by January 1724, firmly in control of Sudbury's town government, he decided to force the issue. He hired workmen to tear down the east-side church, and at town meeting he announced that the timbers would be moved to the Ross land site, whether the Rosses agreed or not. A dissenting neighbor, Edward Sherman, stood up and told Jennison that "he had no power to carry timber on to James Ross's land, not yet." But Jennison threatened to "break the bones" of anyone who interfered.

On March 6, 1724, Jennison and his committee led a convoy of ox sleds, laden with church lumber, to the field opposite the Ross house. James Ross Jr. stood there waiting, backed by other Sudbury residents carrying clubs and staves who showed up to defend him. Jennison brought money (approximately fifteen pounds for the half acre of land where he wanted to build the church), but James refused to accept payment and warned Jennison's men "to stand off on their peril." Instead, Jennison's people began pulling down the Ross fence, while James and his friends tried to stop them. One of the fence posts, frozen into the ground, still blocked the way, and Jennison called for an axe to chop it down. James struggled with him, until Jennison knocked James to the ground, brandishing his axe and threatening to "split him." Cooler heads must have prevailed, for James and his supporters backed off while Jennison's workers unloaded the church timber. As soon as they left, James and his friends carried all of the lumber off the property again, and James filed a lawsuit against Jennison in Middlesex County Court for "breach of the peace."

Although the final outcome of that case is not clear, Jennison and his committee never forced James to relinquish his land for a church. Sudbury found a compromise construction site, only a few hundred feet down the road, on the acreage of a more willing landowner, Hopestill Bent. And Jennison's thuggish behavior was not rewarded by his Sudbury neighbors. Voted out of office within the year, Jennison moved west, settling in Worcester, Massachusetts. James Ross Jr. lived out his life on the family land, as did his own son, and the property ultimately passed out of Ross hands with its sale in 1765.

Finally, in 1815, when hardly anyone remembered the Jennisons or Rosses, local leaders looked for a new church site. And this time, again, the town chose land on the old Ross farm. There they raised a new building—today's peaceful First Parish Church—at the very spot where men once raised clubs and axes in an angry standoff.

Chapter 7

SUNDAY MEETING

*Not all colonial New Englanders were piously religious, despite laws requiring
all residents—regardless of their beliefs—to attend the established Puritan
church services. Sunday dissent and disorder occurred with surprising frequency
throughout the 1600s, even though violators were sure to be punished.*

*The first story in this chapter, "The Naked Quaker," reveals the extreme protest
of one bold woman who expressed her contempt for Puritan authorities in
Newbury, Massachusetts—and some less radical (but nonetheless startling)
actions taken by other people to disrupt the seventeenth-century Sabbath. In
"The Harvard Heretic," we see what happened to one of the most important
and respected men in the New England colonies when he dared to question
a basic tenet of Puritan belief.*

THE NAKED QUAKER

One Sunday morning in April 1663, the residents of Newbury,
Massachusetts, took their assigned seats in the local meetinghouse.
Attendance at Sabbath services was required by law in the Puritan
Massachusetts Bay Colony, and some Newbury families trekked miles over
muddy fields and rutted cart paths to arrive at church on time. The weather
was cold and wet, so people undoubtedly bundled up in heavy garments and
shivered in the unheated meetinghouse, waiting for the minister to begin his
sermon. Imagine the congregation's shock when, suddenly, a young woman
walked through the doorway and took off her clothes!

The naked woman, Lydia Wardell, was a Quaker from nearby Hampton,
New Hampshire (a town then under Massachusetts jurisdiction). For years
the Massachusetts authorities had engaged in unrelenting persecution of
Quakers—the General Court issued a series of laws penalizing that "cursed

sect of heretics"—and it was illegal for Quakers to meet together or to teach others about their beliefs. Some Quakers who refused to keep quiet about their beliefs were banished from the colony, and a few were executed. By 1660 the king commanded Massachusetts to cease these extreme punishments, but Quakers still could be fined and disenfranchised for absences from Puritan Sabbath meetings. In fact, at the latest county court session in April 1663, the judges had ordered Lydia and her Quaker husband, Eliakim Wardell, to pay fines for missing church on twenty consecutive Sundays.

Lydia chose a dramatic response—appearing naked at the Newbury meetinghouse—to express her contempt for Puritans who insisted that she attend church contrary to her beliefs, and she certainly managed to get the

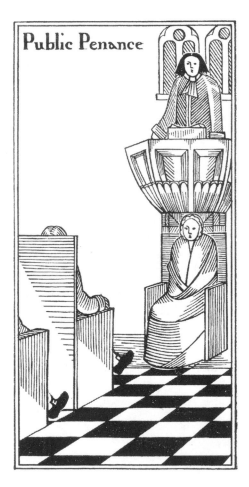

attention of authorities! She was not, however, the first Quaker to try nudity as a protest tactic. The practice was popular among dissenting Quakers (usually men rather than women) in 1650s England, as a way to symbolize the spiritual nakedness of their persecutors. And only a few months before Lydia's act of defiance, Deborah Buffum Wilson, another Quaker woman, had strolled naked through the streets of Salem, accompanied by her mother and sister. (Ironically, although Deborah's nudity offended the authorities, they ordered her whipped while "naked . . . to her waist," and they tied Deborah's mother and sister, also stripped half-naked, on either side of her as the punishment was administered.) Lydia, too, "was ordered to be severely whipped" for her offence, presumably in a similar fashion at the public whipping post.

What made Lydia's nude protest particularly scandalous was the place where she disrobed—at church. Disorderly conduct at Massachusetts churches, while rarely as extreme as Lydia's behavior, was not uncommon in colonial days. Massachusetts officials zealously prosecuted people who interfered with Sabbath services or behaved disrespectfully toward the ministers, but the threat of punishment was never enough to prevent Sunday misbehavior.

Although Quakers tended to stay away from church, suffering fines rather than keeping company with Puritans, other dissenters, such as the Baptists, tried to promote or explain their beliefs. In 1654, for example, Harvard College's president Henry Dunster interrupted a Cambridge religious service to speak out against "corruptions stealing into the Church"—particularly the practice of baptizing infants, which he believed was contrary to biblical teachings—and he attempted a scholarly lecture while the ruling elders shouted him down. Dunster's unorthodox views, and his insistence on voicing them in church, led to court sanctions; Harvard demanded his resignation. (Read more about Dunster later in this chapter.)

Other Massachusetts Baptists (or Anabaptists, as they often were called) challenged infant baptism. Some, like Mr. Townshend Bishop of Salem, or Woburn's Hopestill Foster, attended church but expressed silent disapproval, simply standing up and turning their backs whenever babies were baptized. Christopher Goodwin of Charlestown opted for a more direct approach. During Sunday services in 1663, he jumped up from his seat, grabbed the basin of baptismal water, and dumped it on the floor; then he struck and kicked the constable who tried to subdue him. An unrepentant Goodwin, convicted of "contempt and violence" by the Middlesex County Court, was sentenced to pay a large ten-pound fine or be "openly whipped 10 stripes."

Sometimes people disrupted church by insulting the ministers. Although seventeenth-century Puritan ministers occupied a high social rank—generally they were college-educated, fluent in Latin and Greek, and entitled to use the honorific "Mr." before their names—these churchmen were not always popular. One young Lancaster woman, Mary Gates, was admonished in 1657 for "bold and unbeseeming speeches . . . on the Lords Day and especially against Mr. Rowlandson Minister of God's word." Thomas Oliver's wife went so far as to say "that all ministers in the country were blood-thirsty men," a charge bordering on blasphemy, and she wound up "tied to the [Salem] whipping post with a slit stick on her tongue."

Sunday services lasted six or seven hours, with only a noontime break, and few ministers possessed the oratory skills to compensate for a cold meeting-house and uncomfortable seats. Boring sermons generated many rude comments. Gloucester's Mrs. Holgrave, for example, was fined in 1652 and ordered to make public confession for complaining that minister Perkins "was fitter to be a Ladies Chambermaid than a Preacher." Similarly, at Marblehead in 1654, Elizabeth Legg made a scene at church, reproaching her minister and telling the congregation: "I could have a boy from [Harvard] College that would preach better than Mr. Walton for half the wages." In Charlestown, Ursilla Cole said that she "would as leave hear a cat meow" as listen to the ministers preach, and her insolence was punished with a five-pound fine. Joseph Gatchell mocked Mr. Higginson, the Salem preacher, for "bawl[ing] like a bear," and John Hoar scorned the Concord minister, saying "that the Blessing Master Buckeley pronounced . . . was no better than vain babbling." (Further accounts of John Hoar appear in chapters 6 and 10.) The courts imposed fines for these disrespectful remarks.

Some members of the congregation objected less to the preaching than to the location of their seats. Social rank and age determined seat assignments, and seating disputes triggered Sunday-morning misbehavior. At Newbury in 1669, Elizabeth Randall tried to reclaim an old seat reassigned to others, which the new occupants had renovated as a fancy gated pew. "Although she had been granted another seat superior in dignity," the determined Elizabeth hiked up her skirts and proceeded "to climb, ride or stride over" the tall pew partition, "forc[ing] the door upon the proprietors who were in the seat before her, to the disturbance of the congregation." The Essex County Court admonished her for "disorderly carriage . . . unbecoming her sex." She was not the only Newbury resident dissatisfied with church seating. John Wolcott threatened an appeal to the Massachusetts General Court for loss of his favorite seat, and he vowed that "if he could not sit in that seat, he would cut it down."

Personal conflicts sometimes flared up in violence at church. Robert Beachem of Ipswich, for example, lost his temper during services in 1651, "striking Joseph Fouler with his elbow on his breast, and calling him saucy rascal, with other bad language." Thomas Browning received twenty lashes in 1658 for "striking and fighting in Watertown meeting house in the time of public exercise." In 1670 John Clark even attempted murder "on the Lord's day in sermon time, thrusting a knife against the ribs of Jestin John, saying if his knife had been sharp enough he would have thrust it into his body."

Puritan youth behaved no better at church than their elders. Springfield's Joseph Leonard and Samuel Harmon, for example, amused themselves in 1661 by knocking off hats, "whip[ping] and whisk[ing] one another with a stick . . . in sermon time," and squeezing poor Jonathan Morgan until he cried. In 1670 at Ipswich, the Cogswell brothers taunted Thomas Bragg about his new hat, telling Thomas "that he was not such a pretty fellow," and finally provoking the normally mild-mannered lad to "hit Edward Cogswell, beat his head against the wall and ma[k]e the blood fly out of his nose." Young Thomas Mentor also "carried himself very irreverently and unchristianlike . . . in the time of worship," laughing, talking, and disturbing other children by "snatching away their posies . . . from their bosoms." William Whitred, John Peirce, and John Knoulton disrupted Ipswich meetings "by prating together," or "spitting in one another's faces, pricking one another's legs, 'justing' boys off their seats, heaving things into the other gallery among the girls who sat there and breaking the glass windows." Boys were not the only offenders. Teenagers Elizabeth Hunt and Abigail Burnam spent most Sunday meetings pushing and shoving each other with their chairs.

Why were Sunday disruptions so common in a strict Puritan culture where religion played such a central role? Mandatory church attendance and limited opportunities for protest undoubtedly prompted some of the rebellious conduct. Whatever the reasons for misbehavior "in sermon time," Massachusetts Puritans never stopped trying to enforce Sabbath piety. Naked Quakers, and others who violated the sanctity of the Sunday meetinghouse, were sure to be punished.

Lydia Wardell and her husband evidently realized that continued resistance to Puritan authority would be futile—she never tried taking her clothes off again in church—but the Wardells refused to give up their Quaker beliefs. Not long after her whipping, Lydia and Eliakim fled to the tolerant refuge of Newport, Rhode Island. By 1665 the Wardells, with seven other Quaker families, founded the town of Shrewsbury in the New Jersey wilderness— where the Puritan persecutions became a distant memory, and they could worship as they pleased.

THE HARVARD HERETIC

In November 1654, as the night watchman made his rounds through the streets of Cambridge, Massachusetts, candlelight still flickered inside the big house next to Harvard College. There, at the president's residence, sat Henry Dunster, close to the hearth to keep his ink from freezing; the only sounds were the scratch of his quill pen against parchment and the raspy coughs of his sick wife and child in their bedchamber across the hall. Instead of preparing the next day's Latin lecture for his Harvard scholars, as Dunster normally spent his evenings, he was composing a petition to the Massachusetts General Court. After years of devoted service as the respected head of this first American college, Dunster was no longer Harvard's president; he had been forced to resign, and he was threatened with banishment from the colony in a matter of days. Worried about his bleak future prospects, Dunster wrote one final humiliating appeal to the magistrates, begging to be allowed to stay in the house through the coming winter, until he could settle his family elsewhere.

Fourteen years earlier, when Dunster arrived in Boston as an earnest young graduate of England's Cambridge University, no one could have predicted

Henry Dunster's handwritten notes from *A Concent of Scripture*, a book in his personal library.

the astounding rise—and fall—of his fortunes in the Massachusetts Bay Colony. In 1640 brand-new Harvard College needed a professor, and Dunster's mastery of Latin, Greek, Hebrew, and other arcane scholarly subjects came to the attention of Puritan authorities. Despite Dunster's inexperience (he had worked only briefly as a schoolmaster in England), he soon found himself installed as Harvard's first president and sole instructor. He married a wealthy widow (acquiring stepchildren and the colony's first printing press), married again when his first wife died, and began raising a family of his own, all while turning Harvard into a first-class educational institution comparable to the best colleges in the Old World.

Under Dunster's energetic leadership, Harvard thrived, and he might have stayed on as president for life, if only he had not chosen to question one of the basic tenets of Puritan belief. Ironically, the very qualities that served him well as the scholarly head of Harvard—intellectual curiosity, outspoken honesty, and a love of debate—led to his downfall.

The subject that so inflamed Puritan authorities and triggered Dunster's soul-searching was infant baptism. Established church doctrine required that children be baptized shortly after birth, and parents could be punished for failing to do so. In England and the colonies, however, Baptists, or Anabaptists, began questioning the theological validity of infant baptism. Should all people, they argued, have the opportunity to decide for themselves whether to make a commitment to God through baptism? Why should parents make this decision for children, who could not yet speak for themselves? Should baptism be reserved for adults who freely chose the rite?

These questions set off a firestorm of controversy, and Puritan Massachusetts reacted with fear and heavy-handed persecution, determined to prevent the Baptist contagion from spreading. In 1651 a notorious court case focused public attention on the Baptists and their beliefs. Three men— a minister, John Clarke, a preacher, Obadiah Holmes, and John Crandall, all members of a Baptist church in Newport, Rhode Island—dared to cross the border into Massachusetts for a visit to the blind and aged William Witter of Lynn. At Witter's invitation, they conducted a worship service and baptized several converts in his home, before a constable came to arrest them. At a trial in Boston, Governor Endicott raged that the Rhode Island Baptists "deserved death," but he sentenced them to heavy fines "or to be well whipped." Compassionate friends paid the fines for Clarke and Crandall, but Holmes declined payment of his fine and received thirty lashes at the whipping post, a near-killing punishment that left him severely injured. Rather than quelling dissent about infant baptism, however, that brutal beating gained new sympathizers for the Baptist cause and led Dunster to a crisis of conscience.

Ever the scholar, Dunster plunged into intensive research about baptism, rereading the Bible and the writings of noted theologians. To Dunster's surprise, he could find no scriptural support for the Puritan insistence on baptizing infants; to the contrary, his analysis convinced him that the only people entitled to baptism were true adult believers. The logical next step, for New England's most prominent educator, was to share the results of his research with others. Dunster began by speaking out during sermon time at church, and when his fourth child was born in 1653, Dunster declined to have him baptized.

Anyone else who expressed open opposition to infant baptism could have expected arrest and a quick trip to court, but this dissenter was the president of Harvard College. Dunster's unorthodox views presented Puritan authorities with an embarrassing dilemma, and they tried, at first, to handle the matter quietly. The youthful Cambridge minister Jonathan Mitchell paid Dunster a visit, hoping to rescue the good man from his unaccountable lapse of judgment and to set him straight again. Unable to persuade Dunster of his doctrinal errors, however, Mitchell left the meeting with a horrifying suspicion: was the Devil working through Harvard's president?

Mitchell reported his qualms to the Massachusetts Court of Assistants, which responded with an urgent missive to ministers throughout the colony, seeking investigation of Dunster's "practice and opinions against infant baptism." The result was a two-day debate in Boston. Twelve scholarly church leaders lined up against Harvard's president (arguing in the formal syllogistic style they had all learned at college in England), but they could not sway Dunster from his beliefs.

The Puritan authorities dithered, reluctant to fire Dunster but also unwilling to tolerate his dangerous challenge to church doctrine. In May 1654 the General Court declared, in an act obviously aimed at Dunster, that teachers who "have manifested themselves unsound in the faith" should not continue "educating . . . youth . . . in the college." Dunster responded by tendering his resignation from "the place wherein hitherto I have labored with all my heart." The General Court referred the matter to a governing board of college overseers, instructing them to seek a replacement for Dunster if "he persist in his resolution more than one month." They were leaving the door open—giving Dunster one last chance to renounce his heretical opinions.

But Dunster refused to back down. On July 30 he interrupted a baptism ceremony at church, once again trying to explain his views. This disturbance landed Dunster in county court and sealed his fate at Harvard. The college overseers informed Dunster that "the interests of the College and Colony required his removal," and Dunster submitted a second and final resignation on October 24. The overseers immediately offered the presidency (and Dunster's house in Cambridge) to Charles Chauncy, a Plymouth minister who believed in infant baptism.

Although Dunster had built the house mostly at his own expense, Harvard considered the dwelling to be college property. Winter was coming on, and since Dunster had no other home or employment, he petitioned the General Court to be allowed to stay in the house until Harvard had settled his accounts. He also asked permission to support his family by "preaching the Gospel . . . , teaching or training up of youth, or . . . any other laudable or liberal calling as God shall chalk out his way." The magistrates curtly denied Dunster's petition, making it clear that they expected him to leave the colony.

Dunster wrote back, offering to "willingly bow my neck to any yoke of personal self-denial," but "my wife is sick, and my youngest child extremely so, . . . that we dare not carry him out of doors." Dunster also penned these poignant remarks: "The whole transaction of this business . . . , when all things come to mature consideration, may very probably create grief on all sides; yours subsequent, as mine antecedent. I am not the man you take me to be."

This appeal gained Dunster a few extra months in the house—until March 1655—but no further concessions. Driven from Massachusetts, the family settled in more tolerant Plymouth Colony, at Scituate, where Dunster preached sermons in the remaining five years of his life. Before he died, in 1659, Dunster bequeathed some of his books to the Cambridge minister Jonathan Mitchell and to the new Harvard president, Charles Chauncy. Dunster also asked that his body be transported back to Cambridge for burial. Dunster's final resting place is in the Old Burying Ground, just steps away from his beloved Harvard College.

Chapter 8

FRONTIER JUSTICE

Even at the edges of the seventeenth-century Massachusetts wilderness—in New Hampshire and Maine, and along the Connecticut River—transplanted Englishmen quickly established courts modeled on the institutions of the old country. These early courts were surprisingly sophisticated for a rough-hewn society—with jury trials, literate judges, and careful record keeping— although the types of cases sometimes reflected the unruly "wild west" mentality of the people who lived there. The following stories offer a glimpse into life on the long-ago New England frontier.

The first, "Chesley and the 'Cheating Knave,'" takes us to the dangerous world of the early New Hampshire rivers and forests, where a feisty man with a quick temper lands in court—over and over again. Men were not the only unruly and outspoken people on the colonial frontier, however, and in " 'Breaking the King's Peace'" we meet two uninhibited women from Kittery, Maine—Mary Mendum and Joan Andrews. Finally, " 'To Drive Away Melancholy'" shows how one doting colonial husband tried to entertain his young wife during a long winter at their isolated farmhouse.

CHESLEY AND THE "CHEATING KNAVE"

In the mid-1600s Philip Chesley built a house on the banks of the Oyster River (near Dover, at today's Durham, New Hampshire), just a short canoe ride from the sawmill owned by a man named Valentine Hill. Although the Oyster River "plantation" was less than seventy miles from Boston, Chesley's frontier community seemed a world away—at the edge of a wilderness of fast-flowing rivers and virgin forests. Here, and at other sawmill towns along waterways in the Maine and New Hampshire region, men like Chesley felled trees with saws and axes, hauled or floated logs to the mills, and transported the cut boards to harbors and distribution points.

Lumbermen divided their time between communal forest camps and the mill communities where they had settled with their wives and children, supplementing their income with farming, fur trading, fishing, and whatever else they could do to eke out a living.

Few of these colonial jacks-of-all-trades became wealthy, famous, or notorious enough to merit mention in history books, and Philip Chesley was no exception. His life would remain virtually unknown (except, perhaps, to some of his descendants who managed to trace their ancestry), if not for the fact that Chesley was a brash, outspoken, and occasionally violent man whose quick temper often landed him in trouble—and in court. Chesley's legal problems occupied colonial judges for decades, and the surviving court records reveal much about the personality of this feisty man and the dangers of life on the early New England frontier.

Although settled communities like Oyster River offered colonists some measure of safety and security—with courts and constables to maintain order and friends to lend a hand—life in seventeenth-century New Hampshire remained perilous, the future always uncertain. Indians posed no serious threat in the early years of the colony, but the very forests and rivers that afforded men their living could also mean death, sometimes in an instant. Accidents killed even the most experienced frontiersmen. On December 26, 1660, for instance, when Chesley was serving as local constable, he had the sad duty of convening neighbors for an inquest "to view and take notice of the sudden death of Thomas Canyda." A massive tree fell on Canyda—perhaps he tripped as he lunged out of the way, after his final axe stroke—and men had to saw through the trunk to reach Canyda's lifeless body. Drownings took men just as unexpectedly. In 1657 Chesley served on a jury, finding that "Robert Champion was drowned by accident." And Chesley's testimony appears in the court records of another drowning case, that of his Oyster River friend Alexander MacDaniel, a Scotsman. MacDaniel might have had a premonition of his death, because in January 1664 he told Chesley "that if he died, he would give all that he had to his cousin John Roy." Ten days later, MacDaniel drowned somewhere between York and Dover.

Chesley was one of the lucky ones, living to old age despite the many hazards of the New Hampshire frontier, perhaps because he was quick to react when danger came his way. Although acting on instinct, without taking time

Seventeenth-century lumberjacks felling a mast tree.

to think, may be a useful wilderness survival mechanism, such impulsivity does not necessarily lead to harmony in personal and business relationships. As the court records make painfully clear, Chesley's long life was punctuated by problems with other people, difficulties that he caused—at least in part—by lashing out too swiftly with fist or tongue.

He could not get along with his wife. In the summer of 1646, for example, the county court fined Chesley for "beating his wife and for many bad speeches," and again, in 1650, judges scolded the couple for "fighting and brawling." (Some of Chesley's behavior might have stemmed from too much alcohol; at the court session in 1650, he and several of his neighbors were admonished for drinking at the ordinary on Sunday afternoon instead of attending church services.) Chesley's marital relations grew increasingly turbulent, and his wife fled to their neighbor William Beard's house in 1655, claiming that Chesley threatened to break her neck. Chesley apparently ran off as well, triggering a manhunt for one "day and part of a night" by the constable and two deputies, who finally caught up with Chesley and arrested him for "disorderly living with his wife." In court, neighbors from across the river—William Roberts and William Williams—testified that they heard Chesley swearing, "calling God to witness that he would never have any more society with [his wife and] many other vows." The result was a stiff financial penalty; Chesley had to post the large sum of forty pounds as a bond to ensure his future good behavior.

Apparently, this sentence brought some household peace. Chesley and his wife did not return to court after that (although perhaps she died, for genealogical accounts indicate that he married again in the 1660s), but Chesley's words found other targets. Chesley threatened to shoot John Redman, a blacksmith, "to the Devil" and boasted that he would "cut the throat" of another man who angered him. He made "reproachful speeches against the worshipful Captain Wiggin" (probably arguing with Wiggin or disobeying orders during one of the periodic militia training sessions). The court gave Chesley a choice, which could not have been easy for a man like Chesley: either he must make public apologies to Captain Wiggin before the "train band" *and* at meetings in both Dover and Oyster River, or he would be whipped "ten stripes" and fined five pounds.

That punishment was mild, however, compared with the consequences Chesley faced when the merchant Samuel Hall sued him for slander. The controversy began about June 1661 at Chesley's house in Oyster River, where he negotiated a business deal with Hall, a middleman-trader who boasted of "considerable dealings in . . . merchandise for England, Barbados and other places." Chesley had furs to sell—beaver and moose (nineteen "mouse" skins, according to the quaint phonetic spelling of the court records)—and Hall had lined up a buyer. The deal required travel: Hall gave Chesley a down payment there in Oyster River; Chesley loaded the beaver and moose skins on a ship and promised to deliver the pelts in Boston, where the merchant William Kilcupp would weigh them and provide a receipt; and then, finally, at the end of the summer, Hall and Chesley would meet up in Salisbury, Massachusetts, where Hall would pay Chesley the balance of his money (about ten pounds) in exchange for Kilcupp's receipt. But when Chesley showed up as agreed in Salisbury, there was no sign of Hall or his money. Chesley, outraged and convinced that he had been cheated, denounced Hall to anyone who would listen.

Word filtered back to Samuel Hall, who had been much too busy with important business in Boston and other locales to be bothered with traveling to Salisbury to pay his tiny debt to Chesley, which of course he would settle eventually. Hall decided to teach Chesley a lesson. Claiming that his reputation was ruined and that he was "deadly wounded in his credit," Hall sued Chesley in 1662 for slander, demanding damages in the astonishing sum of five hundred pounds, more money than Chesley could ever imagine raising. This excerpt from Hall's long complaint is typical of his florid prose: "No greater injury can be imposed upon a man than to be wounded in his name and credit and to have his name stained. . . . Public slanders spread over all the Country (as lightning from one side of the heavens to another) so that . . . to have his good name stained and taken away . . . is irreparable. No [one] will credit a man [who] is a cheating knave and a cozening knave."

The extant legal records show how seriously seventeenth-century courts viewed slander allegations, even in the rowdy environs of a New England colonial frontier. Constables attached Chesley's assets, tying up all his land

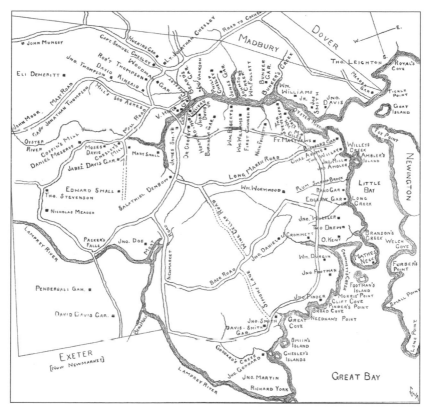

Map of Oyster River Plantation, New Hampshire

and property holdings until the lawsuit could be resolved, and other creditors started hounding him, worried that they would never be paid if Hall
won the case. Magistrates took testimony from the numerous people in
New Hampshire and Massachusetts who heard Chesley accuse Hall of being
a "cheating knave." Chesley may have been loudmouthed and volatile—as
one witness, Robert Pike, wryly observed, Chesley "was not backward to
speak," and he "did express himself in terms somewhat of the grosser
sort"—but the local New Hampshire jury had little sympathy for an arrogant outsider like Hall. They returned a verdict against Chesley—conclud-
ing that, technically, he did slander Hall—but instead of five hundred
pounds, the jury decided that Hall's damages were a mere fifty shillings.

This close encounter with financial ruin left Chesley determined to protect
his assets and his family's future. After the slander trial, Chesley deeded all
his property along the Oyster River to his two sons, Thomas and Philip Jr.
(who by then were young men in their late teens), reserving only one room
at the west end of the house for himself. The next time Chesley lost his
temper and wound up in court—and he did, many more times—he would
not risk losing all that he had worked so hard to earn.

For a man like Chesley, land was the only wealth that mattered, the only
lasting legacy he could offer. When he died is not clear (he was living as late
as 1685), but he undoubtedly witnessed the beginnings of the Indian wars,
when Oyster River, and all New England, faced unexpected new dangers. In
1675 and 1694 Native Americans attacked the community, burning Chesley
houses and buildings, but the family—and their landholdings—survived.
Chesley's elder son, Thomas, died when hostile Indians returned in 1697.
Over the years more Indian raids killed several Chesley grandsons and even
a great-grandson. But generations of Chesleys stayed on near the Oyster
River, into the eighteenth and nineteenth centuries, loyal to the home made
possible by their rough frontier ancestor, Philip Chesley.

"BREAKING THE KING'S PEACE"

Maine, by the mid-seventeenth century, was little more than a cluster
of towns perched along rivers, harbors, and coastal islands north of the
Piscataqua River. Courts had been operating there since the 1630s, trying

to impose order and civility, but Maine remained a frontier outpost, independent and hard to govern. And it was not just men who committed crimes and caused problems for authorities. The court records reveal surprising detail about how unruly and outspoken colonial women could be, and two Kittery wives, Mary Mendum and Joan Andrews, are prime examples.

Constables arrested both women in October 1651 and took them to court in Kittery. Mary Mendum did not need to travel far, since the judges apparently gathered at her own house. Her husband, Robert, kept a tavern there, which became the temporary courthouse once or twice a year, and this time a new court recorder, Edward Rishworth, sat at the judges' table. Rishworth opened the court record book to a fresh page and began taking notes when the first case was called, about a Kittery man accused of "feloniously purloining" someone's property.

Then came the second indictment of the day, and Rishworth wrote: "We present Goody Mendum for abusing Mrs. Gullison in words." In seventeenth-century New England, words were dangerous things, and people needed to think twice before speaking, or they might find themselves in court—even for swearing and rudeness. Mary Mendum evidently lost her temper, "cursing and saying the Devil take" her new Kittery neighbors, Hugh Gullison and his wife, probably because they had opened a competing tavern. For her intemperate speech, Goody Mendum was fined five pounds, and a few months later the Gullisons were rewarded with an exclusive license to sell wine and liquor in Kittery, apparently putting Robert Mendum out of business.

Next the judges turned their attention to a more troublesome woman, Joan Andrews, "an infamous scold and a breaker of the peace" charged with "abusing the Governor." Rishworth's notes do not describe this alleged abuse, but whatever Joan did, her misbehavior must have been serious. The court ordered her to pay a forty-shilling fine "or else to receive corporal punishment by having 25 stripes upon the bare skin"—a very severe whipping—and Joan's husband, John, had to post a bond for her future good behavior. But that was not Joan's only offense. At the same court session, she and a married neighbor, John Diamond, were charged with "suspicion of incontinency" (the seventeenth-century code words for sexual relations). Lacking sufficient evidence, the judges nonetheless fined Diamond and issued an "act of separation," ordering the suspected lovers "not to keep company one with another."

Somehow Mary Mendum got mixed up in John Diamond's affairs, too. A few months later, she was fined for assaulting John and his wife, Grace, who complained to the court that "they stand in fear of life." And Mary continued to use her tongue as a weapon. She called the Kittery merchant Nicholas Shapleigh a "base knave" and his wife a "peddler's trull," or whore—insults of the highest order—and she told people that Maine's governor, Edward Godfrey, was "a dissembling man." The judges ordered her to make public apologies.

Mary also tangled with Joan Andrews, although Joan apparently initiated their conflict. At the March 1652 court session in York, judges convicted Joan of being a "Make bayte" and for "abusing Goody Mendum" with "many approbrious speeches," including the accusation that Mary was an "Indian whore." (Evidently Joan knew about Mary's conviction, thirteen years earlier in the Plymouth Colony, when she was whipped through the streets of Duxbury and sentenced to wear the letters "AD" on her sleeve as a badge of shame, for adultery with an Indian.) The court ordered another whipping for Joan—"twenty lashes . . . upon the bare skin."

Although Mary disappeared from the court records (perhaps she died), Joan continued her turbulent ways. In 1653 Joan appeared before the judges yet again, sued by Rice Thomas, a Kittery brewer, for slander, assault, and battery. She argued with a grand jury man in court, giving him "many threatening and reviling speeches." And Joan cheated Nicholas Davis by selling him butter with stones in it (apparently to increase the weight of the butter, and thus its price). Since Joan admitted her guilt, she was not whipped this time, but her husband had to post another bond, and the court ordered public humiliation for Joan: to "stand in a town meeting at York and in a town meeting at Kittery till 2 Hours be expired with her offense written upon a paper in Capital Letters pinned upon her forehead."

The next year Joan faced new charges. Mary Hayles accused Joan of "stealing certain things," and Joan responded with a melodramatic courtroom outburst, denying her guilt and calling upon the Earth to "open and swallow her up if she had any goods of Goody Hayles." A few minutes later, evidently

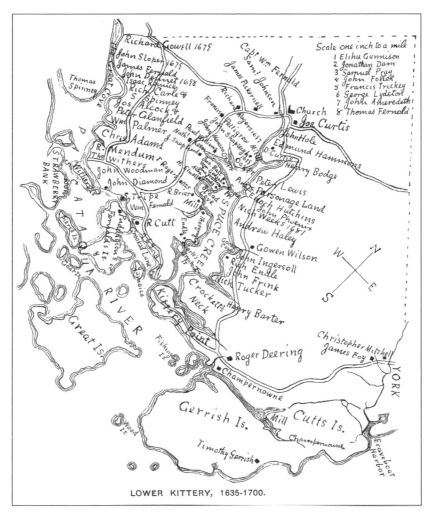

Map of Lower Kittery, Maine, 1635-1700. John and Joan Adrews lived near Christopher Mitchell, along Braveboat Harbor.

realizing that the case was not going well for her, Joan confessed. The court ordered Joan (or her husband) to pay Mary Hayles restitution for the stolen goods, plus fines for stealing, "cursing herself," and "telling a lie."

Life seemed to settle down temporarily for Joan, but soon she and her family found themselves back in trouble. In 1657 the county court at York prosecuted Joan's children, Sarah and Joan, for breaking into the house of the millwright Robert Wadleigh. Joan's husband, John, asked Wadleigh to drop his complaint against the girls, but when Wadleigh refused, John threatened to "take away his estate and life."

Joan had legal problems of a different sort. Again, as in 1652, her neighbors reported an unseemly friendship between Joan and a local married man, this time Gowan Wilson, "to the great discontent of" Wilson's wife (and probably Joan's husband, as well). Court Recorder Edward Rishworth (who also had become a judge and was quite familiar, by this time, with Joan Andrews), wrote in his record book: "We present Gowan Wilson for frequenting the house of John Andrews suspiciously at unseasonable times and for his daily accompanying . . . Joan Andrews up and down Piscataqua River about frivolous occasions, whereby the said Wilson doth neglect his own wife, children and family." Warned by a grand jury man about "the evil of his way," Wilson was unrepentant, retorting that he would not refrain from visiting the Andrews house unless the court told him to leave. Wilson should not have been surprised, then, when the judges did exactly that: they ordered an "act of separation," forbidding Gowan Wilson and Joan Andrews "to come frequently [or] unseasonably into [each other's] company."

But the court was not finished with Joan. Before she and her family left York to go home, she could not resist telling a few people exactly what she thought of them. Joan threatened Goody White "in a profane manner saying that she would swear her self to the Devil." And Joan even made such crude and disrespectful remarks about the judges that they cited her for "contempt of authority," particularly for "saying she cared not a turd for Rishworth nor any magistrate in the world." An outraged court ordered that Joan "be carried out to the post and . . . have twenty lashes given her on the bare skin," but she received a last-minute reprieve. Someone revealed that Joan "was with child" (whose they did not say), and the judges would not beat a pregnant woman. Instead, they agreed to substitute a five-pound fine for the whipping, and to give the long-suffering John Andrews three months to pay it on his wife's behalf.

Maybe Joan tried to be a model colonial goodwife after that, or she was too busy tending a new baby to find time for offending neighbors and breaking the law. But Joan was not to be subdued forever. Although her trips to court diminished, Joan still knew how to offend the authorities. In 1660 she paid a small fine for "being overtaken in drink," and a few years later, in 1666, she was convicted of "breaking the King's peace" by somehow "abusing" Captain Lockwood's wife. This time Joan had no reason to avoid corporal punishment, and she was carried to the post for "10 lashes on the bare skin," administered by York's prison keeper. Perhaps as a reaction to his wife's whipping, John Andrews drank to excess, until he was out of control, shouting insults and blasphemy, hauled back to court as a "high offender against God." According to bystanders, he swore "by the life of God and blood of Christ," and claimed "that he was beyond God and above the Heavens and the stars." When witnesses testified against John in court, he called them names: "dogs, toads and whore's birds." Surely Joan, who was never at a loss for words herself, approved of her husband's sentiments.

By 1671 Joan was a widow—her husband, "by common fame . . . deceased"—and she quickly remarried, to a Kittery fisherman, Philip Atwell. But the marriage was not destined for success. Perhaps Atwell wanted subservience (which Joan's previous husband had learned not to expect), and Joan had no intention of bending her will to any man. She soon kicked Atwell out of the house—sending him, with his belongings packed in a wooden chest, "out into the bushes"—and she resumed the last name Andrews.

"TO DRIVE AWAY MELANCHOLY"

John Henryson spent the winter of 1661–62 with his wife, Martha, in a tiny clapboard house—probably one room with a fireplace (and maybe a loft or kitchen lean-to)—near the town of Springfield. Their farm skirted the edge of the Massachusetts Bay territory, not far from Native American villages, and less than seventy miles from the border with the New Netherlands Colony (today's New York State). They both were young, and Martha had moved up the Connecticut River from Hartford, where her family, the Steeles, still lived. Martha was homesick. She also was pregnant that winter, and as both her condition and the weather made travel difficult, her doting husband looked for ways to keep her entertained.

Sometimes, to wile away those cold winter nights, they played cards together. When Martha did not feel like playing cards herself, she enjoyed seeing John play with his friends. Several times that winter, Springfield neighbors came to the house for card games. They would have gathered around a trestle table, sitting on stools or benches, smoking pipes and drinking beer or cider, while Martha watched from the bed or from a settle (a high-backed wooden bench) close to the fire. Maybe Martha walked around the table, to see who had the best hand, or she cut the cards after someone shuffled them. John was pleased to see Martha laugh and smile.

But no one could quite relax during those sociable evenings, and the Henrysons probably barred the door. If they heard a noise outside, they jumped up to look out the window. They even may have wondered, as they looked around the table, whether they could trust their friends. Why the worry? Because the Puritans considered playing cards, regardless of whether gambling was involved, to be a sinful pastime. And card games were not just a vice for ministers to preach against at Sabbath meeting. What the Henrysons and their friends were doing was against the law, and they could be prosecuted—and punished—in court.

Someone betrayed John and Martha that winter, turning them in to the local authorities. On March 20 Springfield Commissioner John Pynchon called a special court session (with his fellow judges Elizur Holyoke and Samuel Chapin) to hear testimony from the Henrysons and other people accused of "playing . . . that unlawful game of cards" at the Henryson house. Court records do not reveal the informant's identity.

At first, John Henryson may have suspected one of his card partners, Thomas Miller (whom we met in chapter 6). Their relationship had not always been congenial; in fact, only about two years before, Henryson and Miller were decidedly unfriendly, and their enmity spilled over into violence. In 1659 Henryson discovered that Miller had taken or borrowed his cart without per-mission (probably one of those indispensable hand-pulled sledges on wooden runners that colonial farmers often used rather than wagons, for haying and harvesting, moving rocks, hauling dung, and myriad other chores). When Henryson confronted Miller and demanded return of his property, Miller refused to relinquish it, and they quarreled. Miller insulted Henryson, calling him a "Scottish dog" and other "reproachful speeches." Henryson was deter-mined to use force, if necessary, vowing "that either he or Thomas Miller should die before [Miller] should have the cart," and Miller punched him in the face, making his mouth bleed. Both men wound up in court, fined for "hot words and . . . breaking the peace," but Miller had to pay more for causing bloodshed. Although they managed to become "somewhat reconciled" after that, and Miller joined in the card games, Henryson may have wondered whether his neighbor still bore him a grudge.

Or was William Brookes the informant? He was the first to testify at the March 1662 court session, and he identified the card players (implying, however, that he was merely an innocent bystander). "One night at John

Excerpt from March 1662 court manuscript about
"playing at that unlawful game of cards" in Springfield, Massachusetts.

Henryson's house," he said, "[I] saw Edward Foster, Thomas Miller, John Bag and John Scot—all four of them—playing at cards, and I staying in the house near an hour, they continued their play at cards all the while." Brookes, however, had a reputation for dishonesty (sentenced, a few years earlier, "for defrauding sundry persons"), so his testimony alone might not have been enough to convict the card players.

But Edward Foster (who happened to be Judge Holyoke's former servant) spoke next, and he confessed: "It is true. I did . . . play." Foster tried to minimize his involvement, suggesting that more experienced players lured him to the game—"I am but a beginner to play at cards," he said. And Foster made sure that he would not be the only one punished. Like Brookes, he identified his partners in crime: "John Scot, John Bag and Thomas Miller played with [me] at John Henryson's house that night which William Brookes came thither."

At this point, the judges turned to the other accused players—Scot, Bag, and Miller—and what else could they do? They all confessed.

John Henryson had his turn to speak, and he expressed some slight con-fusion about the legalities of card playing—"I did not so well know the Law"—but "it is true, they did play at cards at my house," he said. He also acknowledged playing cards at home on several other occasions, although he would not say with whom. And Henryson added this sweetly poignant defense: "I was willing to have recreation for my wife to drive away melancholy—willing to [do] anything when [she] was ill to make her merry."

Martha Henryson, questioned next by the judges, admitted that she had brought "cards . . . up from Hartford with her," and that she allowed peo-ple to play with those cards at her house. Her husband, however, perhaps hoping to deflect blame away from his wife, stood up to say that he was the one who "had brought her up a pack of cards."

Now one of the confessed card players, John Bag, decided to say more. Maybe he believed that further incriminating Martha would reduce his own punishment (or maybe he was the original informant); in any case, he wanted the court to know that Martha's guilt went beyond simply possess-ing a pack of cards. Bag got up and testified that "he had seen her *play* at cards," too. Questioned again, Martha confessed.

And Martha faced yet more trouble. Two other Springfield witnesses—John Lamb and his wife, Joanna—stepped forward to give testimony against her. Recently, they said, after hearing some rumors, "they asked Goodwife Henryson concerning her playing at cards, and she denied it." The Lambs also reported hearing Martha Henryson say "that she never saw any cards but once at a pinnace and . . . that she brought up no cards to this town all [of] which . . . appears to be a most gross lie."

The court was ready to punish the card-playing wrongdoers. First, they fined Thomas Miller, John Bag, John Scot, Edward Foster, and Martha Henryson five shillings each for "playing at cards." And, although Martha admitted in court, under oath, that she owned and played cards, the judges decided to penalize her for the out-of-court falsehoods, and they ordered an additional "ten shillings for her lie." John Henryson had to pay the highest amount—twenty shillings for "suffer[ing] that unlawful game of cards to be played in his house." William Brookes received no fine, not even a reprimand for lingering at the Henryson house during the unlawful card games, so maybe he was the informant, after all.

Springfield authorities continued their campaign to stamp out card playing in town. Later in 1662 they fined yet another resident, John Stewart, a Scotsman who hosted games at his house—and the informants in that case were John Bag and Thomas Miller. The Henrysons, however, did not stay long in the community. Perhaps John doubted whether Springfield would ever be the sort of town where Martha would feel "merry," so within the year they moved far away, joining a group of twenty-seven other families to settle the new town of Haddam, Connecticut. Martha probably could not play cards legally there, either, but frontier Haddam turned out to be a far safer place to raise their five children than Springfield would have been; in 1675 most of Springfield was burned to the ground when Indians attacked during King Philip's War.

As the years went by, however, Martha apparently still longed for Hartford, Connecticut, her childhood home. The Henrysons relocated to Hartford by 1687, and Martha joined a church congregation there, with four of her children. John did not live long after that—he died in 1688—but perhaps, with the move back to Hartford, he achieved his goal—to drive away Martha's melancholy and, finally, to see her "merry."

Chapter 9

OFFSHORE ANTICS

Colonial New England's economy depended on the sea, and early courts tried to impose law and order offshore, as well as on land. The following stories reveal two different maritime worlds—of privateers and traders who spent most of their time on ships, and of islanders who lived in a semilawless realm that mainlanders never quite managed to control. "The Captured Fortune" *highlights a surprisingly multicultural dispute in Rhode Island—of an English privateer who seizes a Spanish ship near Cuba, brings his prize to Newport, and battles a Jewish Jamaican trader in court. In the second story, "Smuttynose Sailors and Sinners," we focus on the career of one particular sailor and sinner, Roger Kelly, who reigned supreme at the seventeenth-century Isles of Shoals.*

THE CAPTURED *FORTUNE*

In 1744 a motley group of seafaring men—English mariners, French and Spanish sailors, Jamaican Jews, African slaves—gathered outside the royal Court of Vice Admiralty in Newport, Rhode Island. They all awaited the fate of a sloop named *Fortune,* which lay at anchor in the harbor. An English Captain, James Allen, had captured the *Fortune* in Cuban waters after a gun battle with his man-of-war *Revenge,* and now he claimed the aptly named *Fortune* as a prize.

Captain Allen was a privateer, not much different from a pirate, except that he worked legally under commission by the English Crown, seizing enemy merchant vessels up and down the colonial coasts. Before he could collect his lawful share of the *Fortune*'s bounty, however, he needed to prove his claim in court. At Newport Captain Allen petitioned the Court of Vice Admiralty—probably at the elegant brick Colony House, Rhode Island's first government building—for "condemnation" of the *Fortune* and forfeiture of its rich cargo—gold, silver, guns, hides, and slaves (three Africans, named

Buay, Bentura, and Jack). The records of this colorful case—*Revenge v. Fortune*—offer a glimpse into the dangerous and cosmopolitan world of colonial shipping.

Judge Leonard Lockman commenced the admiralty session by calling Captain Allen to his court chambers for private interrogation. Allen testified about his dramatic encounter with two suspicious sloops outside Havana. The *Revenge* "gave chase . . . [but] they did not run," so Allen raised his English colors and approached for a closer look, noticing that one ship, the *Fortune,* flew a Dutch flag. Since the Dutch and English supposedly were friendly at that time, Captain Allen did not expect what happened next.

All of a sudden, "both [sloops] fired upon me," Captain Allen told the judge, "and at the second or third Shot . . . my gunner was killed and each of them immediately poured in their Broadsides upon me." Despite the loss of his gunner and damage to the *Revenge,* Captain Allen managed to overpower the attackers, forcing the *Fortune* to surrender, while the other ship escaped. The *Fortune*'s crew tried to destroy the ship's papers, tossing packets overboard from the cabin window, but waves carried the papers alongside the *Revenge,* and Allen's men fished them out. Those documents, which Captain Allen presented to Judge Lockman, showed that the *Fortune*'s Dutch colors were a ruse: an enemy Spaniard owned the sloop.

The judge wanted to hear from other witnesses before awarding the *Fortune* to Captain Allen. Daniel Pichot, the sloop's shipping master, claimed that he was French and could not speak English, so Judge Lockman summoned an interpreter. Pichot testified that his employer was a Frenchman—not a Spaniard—from the Dutch Caribbean island of Curaçao. The translator switched to Spanish for crew members who followed Pichot, and they offered conflicting opinions about the shipowner's nationality and residence.

Finally, an English-speaking witness, the *Fortune*'s pilot, Thomas Bell, said that the ship belonged to a Spaniard who lived in Spanish Cuba, evidence that Judge Lockman apparently believed. Bell's testimony also illustrated the ephemeral nature of eighteenth-century colonial fortunes. Although Bell had once been a Boston merchant and shipowner himself, he lost everything when his vessel was captured in the Bay of Honduras. Imprisoned by the Spanish in Mexico and eventually released to serve on a French vessel, Bell wound up in Havana, hired by the *Fortune*'s Spanish owner to labor for sixteen "pieces of eight."

Bell described preparations for the *Fortune*'s fateful voyage, helping his employer to fill bags with money, which they loaded into a chest and stowed below decks. As the sloop sailed through Havana's harbor, a small boat rowed over, and Spanish soldiers brought "three Jews" aboard the *Fortune*, paroled prisoners from Cuba's Morro Castle, carrying "with them one chest and a bed tied up in a mat." The Jewish passengers were barely settled into the sloop when the *Fortune* encountered the *Revenge*, and the gun battle began.

When it was clear that the *Fortune* would have to surrender, all on board were in a panic, fearing imprisonment and loss of their valuables—except for one of the Jewish men. Isaac Mendez, son of a prosperous Jamaican Jewish merchant, caught sight of the *Revenge*'s captain and believed that he was a privateer who traded with his father. Mendez figured that he could use his influential Caribbean connections to negotiate fair treatment for passengers and crew when the *Fortune* surrendered, and he promised to secure their possessions in the meantime. According to Thomas Bell, the *Fortune*'s pilot, people began handing Mendez their bags of gold, silver, and other valuables for safekeeping as the *Revenge* approached.

Isaac Mendez was wrong about the privateer's identity; Captain Allen was not a friend of his father's, after all, and Allen seized Mendez's chest with the rest of the ship's cargo. At the Court of Vice Admiralty in Newport, however, Mendez stepped up to Judge Lockman and filed his own claim, identifying himself as a fellow English subject and challenging Captain Allen for possession of the chest's contents. Mendez swore an oath to tell the truth "on the five books of Moses" and requested the return of his property: a gold neck buckle and rings, a pair of "Scissors overlaid with Silver," "one pair of stone sleeve buttons set in silver," and "sixteen hundred and twenty milled pieces of Eight."

Mendez knew people in Rhode Island who could vouch for him. Captain John Beard of Newport took the stand and told of his thirty-year acquaintance with Mendez's father in Jamaica. "I know him to be a man that carries on a considerable trade," Captain Beard reported, "largely on the Spanish Main and to the South Keys." Although Beard did not have "so personal" a relationship with Isaac Mendez, he gave the father high praise: "[He] has the character of a very honest man and I believe his credit would pass equal to any trading man in Jamaica."

Judge Lockman called the other Jewish men, Moses Delyon and Aaron Touro, to his chambers for questioning, and both, like Mendez, swore their oaths "on the five books of Moses." They worked for Mendez and had accompanied him on previous trading voyages, until Spaniards seized their ship at the South Keys and imprisoned them in Havana. While in custody there, Mendez continued active business dealings. Delyon and Touro witnessed many bags of money being delivered to Mendez by his Spanish captors, which they understood were loans (Mendez signed notes and promised repayment) to buy a new ship at Curaçao. According to Delyon and Touro, those loans, not money from the *Fortune*'s passengers, accounted for the large sums in Mendez's chest. The Jewish men also detailed other items in the chest and how Mendez acquired them. The gold buckle, for instance, was a gift from his father, one ring came from Trinidad, and Mendez even purchased rings from the Spaniards during his incarceration at Morro Castle.

The meticulous testimony by Mendez's business associates must have impressed Judge Lockman. He ruled that Mendez had proven his claim to the jewelry, ordering return of the buckle, rings, scissors, and buttons. Judge Lockman, however, still harbored doubts about the money in the chest—those "sixteen hundred and twenty milled pieces of Eight"—so he gave Mendez one year and a day to produce bills and notes proving that he had legally borrowed the money. Otherwise, the pieces of eight would be condemned "as good and lawful prize for the use of the [*Fortune's*] captors." The *Fortune* and its other valuable cargo—including the "3 negro slaves"—were condemned by the Court of Vice Admiralty and awarded to Captain James Allen.

One year and a day later, the deadline expired with no sign of Isaac Mendez, so the pieces of eight from the Jewish chest reverted to Captain Allen. Although Allen and his *Revenge* returned to trolling the coasts, seeking new enemy ships to capture, the *Fortune* case was not over. Soon Captain Allen's own creditors petitioned the admiralty court for a share of the prize, and the captain filed an emergency appeal to Rhode Island's highest judicial body, the Superior Court of Judicature. There the published paper trial ends. Maybe original court manuscripts still exist, filed away somewhere, to tell the rest of the story. But until more records emerge from the archives, we can only guess whether Captain Allen held on to his prize, or whether the captured *Fortune* ever sailed again.

SMUTTYNOSE SAILORS AND SINNERS

Tiny Smuttynose Island straddles the Maine–New Hampshire border, ten miles out to sea from Portsmouth Harbor. Barely a half-mile long and an eighth-mile wide, Smuttynose is uninhabited today. One deserted cottage, a tumbledown cemetery, and ruined stone foundations offer mute evidence, however, that the remote island was not always quiet and empty.

In the seventeenth century hundreds of seafaring men anchored at Smuttynose and other nearby Isles of Shoals during the fishing season. Pirate ships also cruised these isolated waters, and Blackbeard reputedly buried treasure here. Few people resided year-round at the islands in the early days—until the mid 1600s, no women were allowed to live here at all—but, gradually, some fishermen and their families made Smuttynose a permanent home.

Not surprisingly, with its transient sailor population, the Isles of Shoals became notorious for a culture of violence, hard drinking, and fierce independence. Various mainland governments attempted to impose law and order. New Hampshire and Maine (and later Massachusetts, which governed Maine in colonial days) divided up the Isles. Constables arrested wrongdoers and ferried the accused to trial in Dover or York. The authorities even tried holding court on the islands. By 1680 Smuttynose had its own resident magistrate, the fishing master Roger Kelly, who presided at court sessions in his own house, which doubled as the local tavern.

In any other time or place, Kelly would be an unlikely judge. Self-educated and minimally literate, the rough-edged sailor never would have risen to such a position of authority on the mainland. In the semilawless realm of Smuttynose, however, Kelly reigned supreme. He apparently owned most of the island; he also controlled liquor supplies and employed local fishermen.

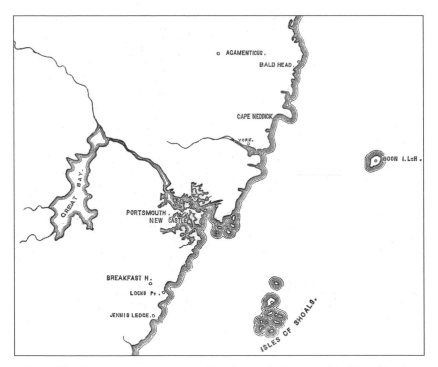

Map of the Maine–New Hampshire coastline, showing the location of the Isles of Shoals.

And he knew the colonial legal system, inside and out. Few people could match Kelly's lurid record of courtroom experience, as litigant *and* as criminal defendant.

Kelly first appeared in the court records as a young sailor in 1664. Accused of "imperiously and illegally" taking over the ketch *Hope* on a voyage to the West Indies (a serious charge in those days of piracy), Kelly spent fifteen weeks in a Boston prison. Finally released, he had barely returned to the Isles of Shoals when he faced new legal problems. This time Kelly was convicted of unlicensed beer and liquor sales at Star Island, just south of Kelly's own Smuttynose. New Hampshire authorities imposed a substantial five-pound fine.

Instead of seeking a legal license, Kelly simply moved his operations north, beyond New Hampshire's jurisdiction, to Hogg Island (today's Appledore). There the Maine authorities caught up with him in 1667. Witnesses testified that Kelly sold to "10 fishermen playing at nine pins on Hogg Island, 12 gallons of wine in one day." This time the penalty was ten pounds, but the magistrates reduced the fine to eight pounds, apparently on the condition that Kelly serve a one-year term as constable for the Isles of Shoals!

This appointment marked Kelly's first stint on the government's side of law enforcement. The constable's job was unpopular and dangerous, more punishment than honor for the hapless officeholder. Hot-tempered Shoalers tended to resist arrest, like the drunken sailor who called Constable Thomas Turpin a "witch, devil, rogue, and diverse other opprobious speeches, and assault[ed] him with many bloody oaths violently." Roger Kelly's constable service was no more peaceful, and in early 1668 he complained of suffering abuse "with words and blows." Bartholomew Burrington "pulled off [Kelly's] neck cloth" and threatened "to break his neck over the Rocks, when the said Kelly had arrested him." Even one of the island women, Rebecha Downes, struck Kelly as he tried to perform his official duties.

A few months later, Kelly was embroiled in lawsuits with other neighbors. At a court session in York, Robert Haines accused Kelly of forcibly taking away his goods, but the jury returned a verdict in Kelly's favor. Kelly and his wife, Mary, were unsuccessful, however, in deflecting complaints about their "abusive carriages," "bad words," and "Ill Counsel." Admonishing the Kellys to "carry it better and . . . to be of good behavior," the mainland magistrates voiced concerns about the couple's "Loose Life."

In the next several years, Kelly was a regular fixture at colonial court sessions, suing and being sued over fishing disputes, trespass, theft, a shoreside fistfight—even a kidnapping case. Kelly continued selling liquor without a license. Yet somehow, despite his "Loose Life" and frequent litigation, Kelly was building up a personal fortune and becoming a man to be reckoned with at the Isles of Shoals. Elected selectman by 1679, Kelly became a member of Maine's General Assembly in 1680 and received his commission as magistrate, to "keep the Courts at the Isles of Shoals, . . . spring and fall." He added "Mr." to his name—a title reserved, in those days, for gentlemen, ministers, and judges.

Despite his growing status, Kelly was not universally popular at the Isles of Shoals. Some people openly defied his authority; Richard Oliver and Robert Mace, for example, abused "Mr. Kelly by very opprobrious language." When Kelly's wife countered Oliver's words with some provocative language of her own—accusing him of murder—she was prosecuted for defamation. Kelly's judicial position did not stop his penchant for lawbreaking, either. Competition in the liquor trade may have triggered one of Kelly's most outrageous scuffles, in 1684, when he and his servant Nicholas Bickeford assaulted the wife of a rival liquor retailer, Phillip Odihorne, kicking her and "dragging . . . her about in an unseemly manner." Although convicted for that brutality, and fined sporadically for unlicensed liquor sales, Kelly nonetheless persisted on the bench, as magistrate or justice of the peace, for most of the years until 1700.

By century's end Kelly was no longer a young man—past seventy and going blind—so he stepped down from his public duties. Still active in the fishing trade, and apparently as cantankerous as ever, Kelly remained at the vortex of trouble. He argued about shipping contracts, and he disputed the title to nearby Malaga Island. A disagreement with his grandson John Frost took a nasty turn in 1705, as described by witnesses at Smuttynose: "John Frost Junior . . . began most horribly to abuse his Grandfather the said Mr Roger Kelly, telling of him he was a false man and his books were false and called his said Grandfather old Rogue and old Atheist and Said . . . Damn your Souls you are all going to the Devil."

Star Island.

Financial quarrels may have prompted this shocking denunciation, but the "Atheist" remark hints at another reason. The Isles of Shoals had never been known for religious piety, but Smuttynose once had its own modest church, with a special "Saints Bell" (donated by a sea captain or pirate). In the years of Roger Kelly's rise to power, churchgoers moved away and ministers stopped visiting, until finally the neglected meetinghouse tumbled to the ground, its rotting timbers pilfered for secular uses. By the early 1700s, a new generation of Isles inhabitants (Kelly's grandson Frost among them) built a church on Star Island, and they wanted the old bell. Kelly, however, refused to part with it (undoubtedly the metal was valuable). Star Island complained to the York magistrates that "Mr Roger Kelly . . . hath now this useless and Silent Saints Bell in his Secret Custody," but the court's resolution is unclear. We may never know whether Kelly allowed anyone, even his own grandson, to hear the bell again.

Roger Kelly's final appearance in the court records—claiming that he was assaulted in his own house by a disgruntled fisherman—paints a rather pitiful picture of the old man but shows that age did not dim his combative spirit. Signing his petition with a shaky but elaborate mark, Kelly alleged that John Deleha grabbed him by his hair and pulled him along the floor, injuring his arm and crippling him. Deleha's version was different: "Old Mr Roger Kelley came out of the other room and stroke me on the head with his cane several blows and broke my head, in the meantime I did endeavor to defend myself." It is a measure of Kelly's feisty reputation that Deleha's story rings true.

Chapter 10

LAWYERS AND JUDGES

As the following stories make clear, trial skills honed in the colonial courts provided upward mobility to a new class of courtroom professionals—lawyers and judges. "The Outspoken Advocate" tells of one farmer-lawyer from Concord, Massachusetts, whose penchant for speaking his mind hindered his success, but the courts could never silence him. One of the most active litigants of the seventeenth century, a jack-of-all-trades who added lawyering and judging to his many talents, is the subject of "Captain Barefoot Goes to Court." And finally, this book ends with a tribute to Magistrate Thomas Danforth, " 'A True New England Man,' " an energetic colonial public servant and life-long Puritan who, despite his flaws, deserves to be ranked with our country's Founding Fathers.

THE OUTSPOKEN ADVOCATE

Nothing intimidated John Hoar—the feisty lawyer spoke his mind no matter how powerful his adversary—but the dangers that he faced one Sunday afternoon in 1676 would make even the bravest man tremble. Hoar had just journeyed sixty miles on horseback, from Boston to the Nipmuck wilderness near Wachusett Mountain, in the midst of King Philip's War. At a time when few colonists dared to venture outside their garrisons, Hoar traveled without military escort, accompanied only by two Christian "Praying Indians," Tom Dublett (Nepanet) and Peter Conway (Tataquinea), who led him to an encampment of enemy sachems. There Hoar expected to argue the most difficult case of his legal career: the ransom of Mary Rowlandson, a minister's wife taken captive nearly three months before in a surprise attack on Lancaster, Massachusetts.

His chances of success did not look promising. As Rowlandson described the greeting Hoar received, the Indians "shot over his horse and under, and before his horse; and they pushed him this way and that way at their pleasure, showing what they could do." At the camp wigwams, Hoar endured days of parley, uncertain whether he was a guest or a prisoner, as painted Indians danced around a cauldron of hot water and threatened to hang him. Finally, Hoar's courage paid off. The sachems convened a general court at a huge granite ledge (known today as Redemption Rock, in Princeton, Massachusetts), where they voted to release Rowlandson for a ransom of twenty pounds. She rode away with Hoar and the two native guides, passing by the charred remains of Lancaster on the way to rejoin her husband in Charlestown.

Hoar returned, with little fanfare, to his family in Concord, Massachusetts. Perhaps the Indians at Redemption Rock admired the fearless Englishman, but John Hoar received no hero's welcome back home. For more than a decade, colonial legal authorities had been punishing Hoar for his outspoken ways, and nothing—not even a daring rescue mission and extraordinary service during wartime—could put him back in Puritan good graces.

We know little of John Hoar's early life, but his courtroom troubles began in the 1660s, when Hoar was filing lawsuits on behalf of his brother, a London trader who believed that his Boston partner was defrauding him. Hoar failed to win any of his cases, and he became convinced that the reason was judicial corruption. He decided to expose the crooked magistrates with a petition to the governor and other high officials, complaining that "he could not obtain justice." The Massachusetts General Court convened a hearing in October 1665. Exactly what evidence Hoar submitted is not clear, but he surely realized that proving the charges would be difficult; almost certainly the magistrates he accused were sitting in judgment against him on the General Court.

Predictably, they "judge[d] his complaints to be groundless and unjust." Instead of simply dismissing Hoar's petition, however, the court announced that Hoar would be punished, to set an example for others who might dare to challenge Puritan authority. Startled and outraged at this turn of events, Hoar stormed out of the courtroom before his sentence could be declared, which only made matters worse. Hauled back to an angry General Court, Hoar learned that he faced imprisonment and a fifty-pound fine, plus a hundred-pound bond "for his good behavior" (enormous sums in those days, the

Redemption Rock, Princeton, Massachusetts.

cost of a house and farm). As if that were not enough, the court also made sure that Hoar would never again scandalize the magistrates: they disbarred him, announcing "that henceforth he shall be disabled to plead any cases but his own in this jurisdiction."

Waiting until tempers had cooled, Hoar approached the General Court again the next spring, asking for relief. The court released his bond and reduced his fine to thirty pounds but refused to rescind the disbarment order. Although Hoar remained unable to pay the lesser fine, the magistrates allowed him to go home to his wife and children in Concord.

If the magistrates assumed that they had silenced Hoar, they were wrong. Back in Concord, Hoar told neighbors at the local tavern that their minister's prayers were "no better than vain babbling." The Middlesex County Court fined Hoar ten pounds for disparaging "the Lord's holy ordinance and making God's ways contemptible and ridiculous." He continued to denounce Puritan authorities until the Court of Assistants finally forced an apology. Hoar submitted a groveling (and perhaps not entirely sincere) request for forgiveness in 1669: "Your humble petitioner . . . humbly . . . cast[s] my self down to your honors feet as in all humility . . . beseeching your honors high Clemency . . . in wisdom and fatherly compassion towards me." Released with a warning never to behave in a "reproachful way" again, Hoar evidently believed that he was free to practice law. Handling a small appeal in county court (for Michael Bacon, accused of stealing swine, as we saw in chapter 6), Hoar could not resist criticizing the judge, and he lost the case, as usual.

When King Philip's War erupted in 1675, Hoar stepped forward to protect sixty friendly Native Americans who lived near Concord. Although authorities interned other Christian Indians on a barren island in Boston Harbor, Hoar invited Concord's Native neighbors to live on his own property. At great personal expense, he built them a workshop and palisade behind his house and helped them harvest their corn. He was unable, however, to stop soldiers who finally came to take these Indians away after the attack on Lancaster.

In the waning days of the war, not long after Hoar secured Mary Rowlandson's release, six Indian women and children were murdered while picking berries in Concord. Hoar's only son, Daniel, was arrested with three other men and convicted of the crime. Whether John Hoar had any role in his son's defense is unclear, but Daniel escaped the gallows with a last-minute pardon, after convincing the General Court that he was not guilty.

When the war ended John Hoar tried to make a fresh start. He returned to the practice of law, but he discovered that the courts still considered him disbarred. In one case after another, judges rejected the papers that he tried to file, "nonsuiting" his clients and saying that he was not a legal attorney. A chastened Hoar tried to make amends, petitioning the General Court in 1680 for release from his disbarment: "I am now grown old, not like long to continue in this world, and loath to leave such a remembrance upon my name or to my children." As a reminder that he had never received thanks for his wartime contributions, he also ventured to ask for "some small parcel of land to comfort my wife with respect unto all her sufferings by my disbursements for the Country." A divided General Court granted Hoar two hundred acres as recompense, but refused—again—to let him work as a lawyer.

Ten years later, Hoar stopped by the courthouse one more time. As Judge Samuel Sewall recalled in his diary: "John Hoar comes into the lobby and says he comes from the Lord, by the Lord, to speak for the Lord; complains that sins as bad as Sodom's found here." John Hoar finally had the last word.

CAPTAIN BAREFOOT GOES TO COURT

One name appears repeatedly in colonial New England court records, Captain Walter Barefoot, a former high seas privateer who arrived in New England by the mid-1600s and settled in Dover, New Hampshire. Like most seventeenth-century gentlemen, the versatile Barefoot plied a variety of trades—merchant, doctor-surgeon, shipowner, sawmill speculator, and Indian trader—and his business affairs inevitably embroiled him in disputes. During the 1660s and 1670s Captain Barefoot showed up at virtually every court session in Maine, New Hampshire, and northern Massachusetts, suing or being sued. The published court records detail nearly 150 cases involving Barefoot in those decades.

Since few people hired attorneys in the seventeenth century, Captain Barefoot generally represented himself, shuttling from one court jurisdiction to another, spring through fall, up and down the New England seacoast. His court travel from fall 1662 through 1663 was typical. In October 1662 Barefoot filed several lawsuits at the county court in Hampton—

suing former patients for unpaid medical bills and complaining that the shipwright Walter Tayler failed to "build . . . a vessel . . . according to dimensions specified." Barefoot did not win any cases at Hampton, but, undaunted, he argued an appeal of the shipwright suit in Boston the following March. Again he lost.

Traveling next to court in Ipswich, the captain posted a bond to ensure the future good behavior of his friend and fellow doctor Henry Greenland (in trouble for "soliciting Mary, wife of John Roffe, to adultery"). Barefoot went to court in Salisbury in April, then to Dover in June, where he won sizable verdicts against debtors for twenty-five pounds in "money or beaver." Two days after the Dover court session, Barefoot was in York, Maine, with suits "for unjustly molesting his person & estate," and for debt, netting judgments of more than ninety-one pounds. He returned to Ipswich in September to testify for Henry Greenland, accused again of "attempting" Goodwife Roffe's "chastity in a foul manner." In late November Captain Barefoot came to Greenland's aid a third time, serving as his attorney in a Salem slander suit for calling someone "a lying knave."

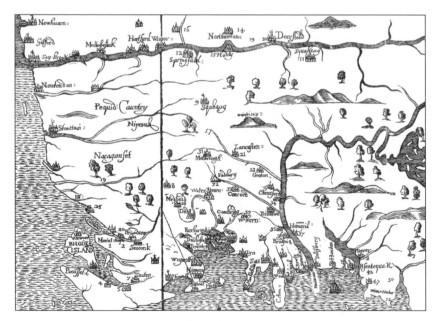

Detail from William Hubbard's 1677 map of New England.

Despite Barefoot's well-practiced courtroom skills, collecting debts from Indians proved particularly difficult. In the summer of 1664 Captain Barefoot sued an Indian named Sesegenaway "for about one hundred skins," but the case went unresolved (probably because Sesegenaway eluded attempts to serve a court summons). Barefoot finally tracked the Indian down at a tavern in Newbury. While his pal Henry Greenland restrained the Indian and sent for a constable, Barefoot sat at a table in the back room, filling out a blank form that he claimed was already signed by New Hampshire court authorities.

A tavern bystander, Richard Dole, questioned the legality of this procedure, but Barefoot told him to mind his own business, or "he would prove [Dole] the verriest knave in New England." Dole retorted, "Captain, do not threaten me, neither to my face nor behind my back," which only made Barefoot escalate his threats. Dole described what happened next: "Captain Barefoot, sitting on the other side of the table said to me, 'Sirrah get ye out of the room [or] I will heave the pot at thy head,' and presently [he] threw the pot and struck me on the head backward to [the] ground." A violent melee erupted. Barefoot responded in swashbuckling style, "his sword drawn, and with high threatenings." Greenland leaped to Barefoot's defense, punching and kicking Dole and other people, and stamping upon the "breast and face" of one tavern patron until he "was all bloody, except his eyes." What happened to the Indian is not clear, but Greenland and Barefoot both ended up in the Ipswich court the next September, fined five pounds each for their "great misdemeanor, endangering . . . lives" at the Newbury tavern, and for resisting arrest.

After the Newbury incident, Captain Barefoot's personal and business relations deteriorated. Barefoot began a long-running feud with Andrew Wiggin, a young man of powerful family connections (son of an influential New Hampshire founder and son-in-law to Massachusetts' Simon Bradstreet). In 1667 Barefoot filed a lawsuit alleging that Wiggin "had abused him by blows and had robbed him of a pistol and several writings" during a roadside scuffle. Although the court concluded that Wiggin did indeed "thrust the said Barefoot into a gully" and fight with him, the judges were less sure about the robbery claim, so Wiggin got off with a small fine for disturbing the peace. Wiggin followed up with his own claim against Barefoot for "high defamation," which he lost and appealed, prompting

Barefoot's countersuit for "molestation" and an astounding one thousand pounds in damages. During a 1668 court session in Hampton, when Barefoot sued Wiggin for debts due in "pine or oak boards" and Wiggin sought possession of Barefoot's sawmill, their enmity degenerated to farce. Approaching Barefoot in the courtroom under pretence of reconciliation, Wiggin "bit him on the face."

Even worse than Wiggin's bite, a series of lawsuits initiated in 1668 by Robert Wadleigh, a millwright, pushed Captain Barefoot to the brink of financial ruin. Barefoot sold Wadleigh a piece of prime sawmill property at New Hampshire's Lamprey River, but other claimants emerged to contest the sale, and Wadleigh demanded that Barefoot make things right. When Barefoot could not clear the title, Wadleigh petitioned the Massachusetts General Court, where Andrew Wiggin's father-in-law, Bradstreet, sat as an assistant. Boston authorities ordered Barefoot to give Wadleigh a "legal conveyance" with a warranty against all claims by others, or else to pay Wadleigh the enormous sum of four hundred pounds.

Captain Barefoot made strenuous efforts to comply with the General Court's ruling and save his fortune—suing the previous owner of the Lamprey River property, while stepping up collection efforts against everyone who owed him money. Word of the captain's financial problems must have spread, however, for Barefoot's creditors filed a flurry of lawsuits and began attaching his assets. After a nasty confrontation with a Boston marshal who seized the captain's ship, the "pinke *Lenham,*" Barefoot found himself in even more serious trouble.

The Massachusetts Court of Assistants decided that New England had seen enough of Captain Barefoot. On March 5, 1672, after fining Barefoot "for his profane and horrid oaths," the court raised startling new allegations—that he had abandoned a wife and two children in England—and "sentence[d] him forthwith to return to England by the first ship." In the meantime, the magistrates barred Captain Barefoot from practicing "Chiurgery or physicke," and as a final slap, they ordered Barefoot to "abstain from [Mrs] Hilton's house at Exeter especially her company." Captain Barefoot, of course, ignored these orders. He returned to New Hampshire, continuing his usual round of lawsuits in the county courts, until marshals from Boston apprehended him again and threw him into prison.

For the next several years, in and out of prison, Barefoot fought back the way he knew best litigating up and down the coast—until fortune finally smiled on the plucky captain once more. Massachusetts lost control over New Hampshire in 1679, and the Boston authorities no longer ruled Captain Barefoot's future. By 1680 he openly practiced medicine again, and soon he found a way to parlay his trial experience into a more prestigious job. On October 5, 1686, when the New Hampshire County Court of Pleas and Sessions convened at Great Island, six men took seats at the judges' platform. One of them was Captain Walter Barefoot.

"A TRUE NEW ENGLAND MAN"

If I could travel back in time somehow to meet just one person in colonial New England, I would choose Thomas Danforth. Anyone who studies Puritan Massachusetts inevitably runs across Danforth's name (which appears numerous times in this book). For fifty years he was at the center of the court, government, and college business in the Massachusetts Bay Colony, and although he had his faults—his conservative views of Puritan morality do not seem very enlightened today—he was one of the busiest, hardest-working men of his time. He probably used more quill pens than anyone else in seventeenth-century New England!

Danforth, the eldest son of a middle-class yeoman farmer, was not yet in his teens when he emigrated from England to Cambridge, Massachusetts, with his father and siblings in 1635. Orphaned three years later, and having received little formal education, he nonetheless rose rapidly in the colonial social and political hierarchy, thanks to his formidable intelligence, energy, and zeal for public service. A list of his many official positions in Massachusetts over the years is almost exhausting to read: Cambridge selectman,

Thomas Danforth's signature.

1645–71; Cambridge town clerk, 1645–68; treasurer, 1650–68, and steward, 1668–88, of Harvard College; Middlesex County recorder, 1648–86 (and treasurer of the county for several years); Middlesex County Court judge (for decades); representative (deputy), 1657–58, and assistant (magistrate) on the Massachusetts General Court, 1659–78; deputy governor, 1679–86, 1689–92; Council member under the colony's second charter, 1693–99; and judge of the Superior Court of Judicature, 1692–99. If the Massachusetts governor Simon Bradstreet had not lived so long, Danforth almost certainly would have risen to that top post, too. And Danforth's achievements extended far beyond Massachusetts, for he served as commissioner to the United Colonies from 1662 to 1678—leading the United Colonies as president during the critical year of 1675, when King Philip's War threatened the colonists' very survival. After his tenure with the United Colonies, he also governed for many years as president of the District of Maine (then under Massachusetts' jurisdiction), while living in Cambridge and continuing his multiple duties in Massachusetts.

Although an exceptionally active and important public official, Danforth did not spend all of his time at court and in meetings. For many years he was in demand, as well, for his expertise as a land surveyor—which required advanced mathematical skills and equipment—and he apparently enjoyed walking the countryside. As late as 1670 he was so frugal and unpretentious that he *shared* a horse with his brother, the minister Samuel Danforth, who lived in another town.

Hardly any of Danforth's personal papers survive—I still hope that more will emerge one day, perhaps in a forgotten archive or in someone's attic—but countless official documents, particularly court files, bear his meticulous and readable handwriting. Many of these cases (some of which are featured in this book) do not portray Danforth in a particularly favorable light, at least by today's standards. A devoutly religious Puritan, he could be a harsh and intolerant judge.

His opposition to the Quakers was especially severe and unyielding, and he played a continuing role in judicial efforts to stamp out that "cursed sect of heretics." In 1663, for example, as a judge of the Middlesex County Court, Danforth heard the case of Elizabeth Howton, "a vagabond and wandering Quaker" arrested for "bold and impetuous" preaching in the streets of Cambridge. At her trial, Howton was unrepentant, not only criticizing the court for injustice, but also calling Harvard College and its divinity students "a cage of unclean birds." Convicted as a vagrant, Howton received multiple whippings—"10 stripes in the prison house," and more lashes at the border of each town as constables escorted her out of the jurisdiction. At the same court session, Danforth fined Benanuel Bowers for "absenting himself from church and entertaining Quakers twice in his house" in Charlestown. The following year, according to a contemporary account, Danforth purportedly told Wenlock Christison, a convicted Quaker who was about to be lashed: "Wenlock, I am a mortal man, and die I must, and that ere long, and I must appear at the tribunal-seat of Christ, and must give an account for my deeds in the body; and I believe it will be my greatest glory in that day, that I have given my vote for thee to be soundly whipped."

Despite the harsh punishment that Danforth imposed on religious dissenters, some of his fellow English colonists believed that he was too soft hearted with Native Americans. Danforth ardently supported efforts to Christianize his Indian neighbors, and Harvard College became the hub of that missionary work. Since Danforth lived just north of Harvard Yard and maintained near-daily contact with the school in his role as steward, it was inevitable that he found himself working closely with two of the Massachusetts Puritans who devoted much of their life to that cause—the minister John Eliot of Roxbury and his fellow magistrate Daniel Gookin of Cambridge (whom we met in chapter 5). Eliot learned the local Algonquian dialect, preached to Indians, and translated the entire Bible into that language, which was printed at Harvard with the help of a native named Wawaus (who came to be known as "James the Printer"). Settlements of Praying Indians sprang up around New England—funded by donations from England and overseen by Danforth and other commissioners of the United Colonies—as Eliot rode circuit to preach and Gookin presided at Native courts. At Eliot's urging, a few Indians enrolled at Harvard and at the Cambridge grammar school (learning Latin and Greek with their fellow scholars). Danforth apparently boarded some of these Indian students at his own home and took particular interest in one young man, Caleb Cheeschaumuk, the only Native American known to grad-uate from Harvard during those early years (1665). Cheeschaumuk even assisted Danforth with his official duties—either working at Danforth's house or traveling with him on court business—for the Middlesex County Court records reveal the Indian's signature as witness on a will and a prenuptial agreement handled by Danforth.

When King Philip's War erupted in 1675, all Indians became suspect, even the Christian ones, and the Massachusetts General Court ordered the Praying Indians interned on barren Deer Island in Boston Harbor. Despite his high positions on the General Court (and his presidency of the Commissioners of the United Colonies), Danforth found his support for the Christian Indians to be very unpopular in wartime. A February 1676 broadside, posted in Boston by the anonymous A.B.C.D. Society, called Danforth and his friend Gookin "traitors to their king and country" and issued this ominous threat: "As Christians we warn them to prepare for death." Two months later, in the waning days of the war, someone evidently made an attempt on Danforth's life. As he sailed out of Boston Harbor (with Gookin, Eliot, and another official) to visit the Indians on Deer Island, a larger boat rammed theirs, and they came close to drowning. And the following year, Danforth narrowly missed death on the streets of Boston. As a witness testified in court:

> I saw John Jones driving his trucks, whipping his horses which
> caused them to run very furiously; the worshipful Thomas
> Danforth being before the trucks shifted the way several times
> to escape the horses, and I was afraid they would have ran
> over him; but having escaped them, when the said Jones came
> to the wharf where I was, I asked him why he drove his trucks
> so hard to run over people, and told him he had like to have
> ran over Mr. Danforth; he answered it was no matter if Mr.
> Danforth and Major Gookins were both hanged.

No one could prove whether the driver deliberately attempted to kill Danforth or was merely negligent, but the court banned Jones from driving a cart in Boston again, "upon penalty of a severe whipping."

Danforth continued in public life for more than twenty years after that incident, taking part in some of the most important affairs of the colony. As England began to exert greater control over Massachusetts government, Danforth steadfastly opposed any infringements on colonial liberties. He played a leading role in the short (and ultimately doomed) "Glorious Revolution of 1689," a little-known chapter in our country's history that nearly achieved Massachusetts independence a century before the American Revolution. And considering Danforth's prominence in the colony's judicial system, it is not surprising that he helped to bring closure to the most notorious legal controversy of the seventeenth century—the Salem witch trials of 1692.

Although a later fictional treatment of the witchcraft case (Arthur Miller's play *The Crucible*) suggests that Danforth was a primary inquisitor, his official involvement actually was minimal at first, since the trials started outside his home county. Not until early 1693, after most of the arrests had been made—and many convicted witches already executed by hanging—was Danforth appointed (with four other judges) to a special court by the new royal governor, William Phipps, to handle the remaining cases.

Danforth, like most New Englanders, still believed in the Devil and witches, just as he had in 1659 at the beginning of his judicial career, when his neighbors Winifred and Mary Holman were accused of witchcraft (see chapter 1). But perhaps he had learned from that earlier experience to be more skeptical of witchcraft claims, particularly those based on so-called spectral evidence, whereby witnesses testified that the accused appeared in supernatural form, rather than in person. According to some accounts, Danforth worked behind the scenes with others, such as Harvard's president, the minister Increase Mather, urging that spectral evidence be banned in the witchcraft cases. When Governor Phipps established the new court, he prohibited spectral evidence, and Danforth, with the other judges, quickly released most of the defendants in witchcraft cases still pending.

Handbill of the A.B.C.D. Society threatening the lives
of Thomas Danforth and Daniel Gookin.

In the case of a Reading widow, Lydia Dustin, however, Danforth reportedly worried that the evidence against her was more than spectral. A contemporary quoted Danforth as warning Dustin, "Woman, woman, repent! There are shrewd things come in against you." Despite his reservations, Danforth nonetheless joined the rest of the court in confirming the jury's not-guilty verdict and ordering her freed upon payment of court fees. Unable to afford the fees, however, Dustin went back to prison until someone could pay them for her, and she died there before she could be released.

In the remaining years of his life, Danforth evidently brooded over the Salem witchcraft trials and his role as a judge and member of the government during this dark and terrible episode. And he was not the only one troubled by these memories. Five years later, in 1697, Massachusetts proclaimed a day of public fasting, to acknowledge the great wrongs done to the victims of the trials. One of Danforth's colleagues on the witchcraft court, Judge Samuel Sewall, stood up that day during services at the South Church in Boston and asked the minister to read his apology to the congregation, accepting "blame and shame" for his part in the trials. Danforth, too, tried to make amends, but in a different way. He presented more than eight hundred acres of his own land, in what is now Framingham, Massachusetts, to families of the victims (who built houses there and called the neighborhood "Salem End").

On a Sunday afternoon, November 5, 1699, Thomas Danforth died of a fever. He was seventy-six years old. His friend and fellow judge Samuel Sewall mourned in his diary: "[He was] a magistrate forty years, . . . a very good husbandman and a very good Christian. . . . Indeed it is awful, that while we are sitting [in court], at the same time the ancientest Judge should be lying by the wall dead in his house." Sewall also wrote, in a letter to a friend, that Danforth was "one of the true New England men," and "a great deal of the first ways of New England [are] buried with him." Though much had changed since the first settlers arrived in New England, and Puritan ideals no longer held sway, Danforth's devoted service as "a magistrate forty years" laid the foundations for the free United States that emerged in the next century. We have Thomas Danforth to thank, perhaps as much as any of the later Founding Fathers, for our American courts and law today.

NOTES

As indicated below, many of the stories in this book are adapted from my "Tales from the Courthouse" column in *New England Ancestors* magazine, a publication of the New England Historic Genealogical Society in Boston. For more information about *New England Ancestors* and the New England Historic Genealogical Society, please visit www.NewEnglandAncestors.org.

The following notes, listed by page number, give short citations of works that appear with full publication information in the bibliography.

CHAPTER 1. WITCHES AND WILD WOMEN

1   "The Witch at the Top of the Stairs": This story previously appeared in Diane Rapaport, "Tales from the Courthouse: The Witch at the Top of the Stairs," *New England Ancestors* 7 (Summer 2006): 51–52. The court records about this case have been published in Dexter, *Ancient Town Records,* 1:249–52, 256–57, 281; Hall, *Witch-Hunting in Seventeenth-Century New England,* 61–73; Hoadly, *Records of the Colony or Jurisdiction of New Haven,* 29–37, 151–52, 497–98. For other information about the Godman and Goodyear families, see Savage, *Genealogical Dictionary,* 2:278, 3:48–49.

2   "Stephen Goodyear and his family": In 1645 the first Mrs. Goodyear was lost at sea on an ill-fated voyage to London. Stephen Goodyear soon remarried, to Margaret Lehen, widow of George Lamberton (who had sailed on the same missing ship). See Savage, *Genealogical Dictionary,* 2:278, 3:48–49.

"a woman of high social rank": I am indebted to two readers of my *New England Ancestors* column—John Brandon and Nat Taylor—who provided these additional clues to Elizabeth Godman's background in England. She apparently was baptized in Sussex about the year 1600, the daughter of Thomas and Mary (Porter) Godman of Ote Hall, Wivelsfield, Sussex, and granddaughter of Richard and Jane (Whitfield) Porter. If this genealogical link is correct, Mrs. Godman was related (as first cousin once removed) to a prominent New England minister, Henry Whitfield, who settled in 1637 at Guilford, Connecticut, and went back to England in 1650. Perhaps she originally came to New England with him, and maybe that relationship helped to save Mrs. Godman from execution as a witch. See Hoadly, *Records of the Colony or Jurisdiction of New Haven,* 497–98; Godman, *Some Account of the Family of Godman,* 42–43. Elizabeth Godman's abrasive personality got her into trouble with the courts before she emigrated. As stated in the "Notes from the Act Books of the Archdeaconry Court at Lewes," *Sussex Archaeological Collections* 49, no. 62 (1906): 1634, "October 21. Wivelsfield. Elizabeth Godman [was censured] 'for pulling downe the May boughes, in a rude scornfull manner, which were brought into the churche to adorn it.'"

"before her name": Whether Mrs. Godman ever married is unknown.

5   "escaped the gallows": Although Elizabeth Godman escaped the gallows, other accused "witches" were not so fortunate. Between 1638 and 1691 there were eleven to seventeen executions in New England; an exact figure cannot be determined because of gaps in the trial records. During the 1692 Salem witchcraft crisis, nineteen people were hanged and one (a man named Giles Corey) was pressed to death. (Thanks to Marilynne K. Roach, author of *The Salem Witch Trials,* for providing this information.)

5   "Watching Widow Holman": The court records about this case, at the Judicial
     Archives/Massachusetts Archives, include Middlesex County (Massachusetts) Court
     Folio Collection, Folio 25, Group 1B, *Holman v. Gibson,* et al. Portions of these
     records also have been published in Hall, *Witch-Hunting in Seventeenth-Century New
     England,* 134–46; Paige, *History of Cambridge,* 356–64. For additional information
     about this case and the families involved, see Paige, *History of Cambridge,* 530, 558,
     587–88, 660; Thompson, *Cambridge Cameos,* 87–97.

     "a newly elected judge": Thomas Danforth was elected as one of the assistants to the
     Massachusetts General Court in 1659, a position with legislative as well as judicial
     duties. The assistants also served as judges (or magistrates) on the Massachusetts
     Court of Assistants and for the county courts where they lived. Danforth, as a resi-
     dent of Cambridge, served as a judge for the Middlesex County Court. Danforth
     reappears in chapters 2, 3, 6, and, especially, 10.

6   "'find out Mrs. Holman'": See notes of testimony in the case in Hall, *Witch-Hunting in
     Seventeenth-Century New England,* 137.

7   "Mrs. Holman was a widow": Widow Holman was referred to in court records as
     "Mrs." Holman, whereas John Gibson's wife appeared as "Goodwife" or "Goody"
     Gibson, which suggests that the Gibson family's social rank was lower than that of the
     Holman family.

11   "A Woman of 'Enthusiastical Power'": This story previously appeared in Diane
     Rapaport, "Tales from the Courthouse: The Strange Case of Mary Rosse and her
     'Enthusiastical Power,'" *New England Ancestors* 6 (Holiday 2005): 50–51, and won an
     "Excellence in Writing" award from the International Society of Family History
     Writers and Editors in 2006. Additional sources include Dow, *Records and Files of the
     Quarterly Courts of Essex County,* 3:120–22; Pramberg, "He Led Two Lives," 144–47;
     Shurtleff, *Records of the Colony of New Plymouth,* 113–14; Waggener, "Notes for
     Jonathan Dunham alias Singletary"; Walroth, "Beyond Legal Remedy."

     "in the court records": The Puritan minister Cotton Mather mentioned this case in his
     Magnalia Christi Americana, 2:530. (Many thanks to Marilynne K. Roach, author of *The
     Salem Witch Trials,* for pointing out this additional reference to the case.)

12   "during the mid-1600s": See Rapaport, "Scots for Sale."

CHAPTER 2. COUPLING

15   "The Scottish Rogue": This story previously appeared in Diane Rapaport, "Tales from
     the Courthouse: The Case of the Scottish Rogue," *New England Ancestors* 5 (Holiday
     2004): 57–58, and won an "Excellence in Writing" award from the International
     Society of Family History Writers and Editors in 2005. The relevant court records
     have been published in Dexter, *Ancient Town Records,* 2:99, 117–23, 148–51, 201, 204,
     222–23, 275–76; and Dow, *Records and Files of the Quarterly Courts of Essex County,*
     5:21–22, 8:305–6. Other sources include Bodge, "Soldiers in King Philip's War," 74;
     Hartley, *Ironworks on the Saugus;* Norton, *Founding Mothers and Fathers,* 27–38 (for a dif-
     ferent perspective on the Pinion family); Rapaport, "Scottish Slavery in Seventeenth-
     Century New England"; Rapaport, "Scottish Slaves in Colonial New England";
     Rapaport, "Scots for Sale."

16   "little better than a slave": Patrick Morran's name appears on a transport list of Scots
     shipped to New England on the *John and Sarah,* published in Charles Banks, "Scotch
     Prisoners Deported to New England by Cromwell, 1651–1652," *Massachusetts
     Historical Proceedings* 61 (October 1927): 17–18; "Scotch Prisoners Sent to
     Massachusetts in 1652, by Order of the English Government," *New England Historical*

and Genealogical Register 1 (1847): 377–79; and *Suffolk Deeds* (Boston: Rockwell and Churchill, 1880–1906), 1:5–6.

16 "Hammersmith Ironworks in Lynn": See Dexter, *Ancient Town Records,* 2:99; and Hartley, *Ironworks on the Saugus.*

20 "The Wandering Wife": This story previously appeared in Diane Rapaport, "Tales from the Courthouse: The Case of the Wandering Wife," *New England Ancestors* 5 (Spring 2004): 54–55. Sources include Dow, *Records and Files of the Quarterly Courts of Essex County,* 2:242–44; 3:192–94, 242; 5:227, 262, 354, 441–42; Essex County Quarterly Court File Papers; Middlesex County (Massachusetts) Court Record Books (1648–63), 1:67.

"'notorious evil carriage'": Undoubtedly, Faith's father knew that Daniel was a Scotsman captured during the English Civil War and transported to colonial servitude in 1651 on the *John and Sarah* with other Scottish war prisoners. Edmond Bridges also may have heard that Daniel was convicted in 1654 for assaulting and beating his Charlestown master. See Middlesex County (Massachusetts) Court Record Books (1648–63), 1:67.

24 "The Rhode Island Runaway": This story previously appeared in Diane Rapaport, "Tales from the Courthouse: The Case of the Rhode Island Runaway," *New England Ancestors* 7 (Spring 2006): 54–55, and won an "Excellence in Writing" award from the International Society of Family History Writers and Editors in 2007. The court records, at the Judicial Archives/Massachusetts Archives, include Middlesex County (Massachusetts) Court Record Books (1648–63), 1:137–38, 166–67, 178; Middlesex County (Massachusetts) Court Folio Collection 16-5, 18 (Group IIIA and Group VG), 1670-55-2, 1672-61-3, 1676-71-2, 1676-72-2, and 55-II-1691. Additional sources include Baldwin, *Michael Bacon and His Descendants;* Bond, *Family Memorials,* 1:393; 2:676; Cutter, *Genealogical and Personal Memoirs,* 2:1141; Nourse, *The Early Records of Lancaster, Massachusetts;* Peirce, *Peirce Genealogy,* 3, 18–27; Savage, *Genealogical Dictionary,* 1:106; *Watertown Records,* 1:48–50, 56–57, 66–67.

CHAPTER 3. PARENTS AND YOUTH

29 "The Prodigal Son": The court records have been published in Dow, *Probate Records of Essex County,* 3:111–18; Dow, *Records and Files of the Quarterly Courts of Essex County,* 2:335, 338, 346; 3:111, 117; 4:37, 175, 297; 5:20, 345–46; 6:233; 9:54–55; Cronin and Noble, *Records of the Court of Assistants,* 3:138–39; Shurtleff, *Records of the Governor and Company,* 4(2):146, 177, 195–97, 209–10, 216–18. Other sources include Kamensky, *Governing the Tongue,* 103–17 (for additional insights about the turbulent Porter family); *The Laws and Liberties of Massachusetts,* s.v. "Capitall Lawes, 14."

34 "Dancing in the 'Night Season'": Court records include manuscripts of Thomas Danforth, quoted courtesy of the Harvard University Archives: Harvard University, Disorders records: examination of College students and others for disorderly conduct, 1676, UAI 15.350.2, Harvard University Archives; Middlesex County (Massachusetts) Court Record Books (1648–63), 1:216; Shurtleff, *Records of the Governor and Company,* 4(1):366; 5:59–63, 131; Wyman, "Abstract of Middlesex Court Files." Other sources include Morison, *Harvard College in the Seventeenth Century; Music in Colonial Massachusetts,* 1:729–38; Paige, *History of Cambridge;* Sibley, *Biographical Sketches of Graduates of Harvard University,* 3:173–77; Thompson, *Cambridge Cameos,* 63, 118–19.

35 "on Brighton Street": Andrew Belcher's ordinary was near the corner of today's JFK and Mt. Auburn Streets in Cambridge, Massachusetts. See Thompson, *Cambridge Cameos,* 63.

35 "the Indian College": This brick building, originally constructed about 1655 to accommodate Native American college students, was by 1660 also used as a dormitory for colonial scholars; it was the site of Harvard's printing press as well. See Morison, *Harvard College in the Seventeenth Century*, 1:340–60.

"King Philip's War": For more information on this conflict, see Schultz and Tougias, *King Philip's War*, and Jill Lepore, *The Name of War*.

"ring in the new year": In 1659 the Massachusetts General Court ordered "that whosoever shall be found observing . . . Christmas . . . , either by forbearing of labor, feasting, or any other way, . . . shall pay . . . five shillings as a fine to the county." Shurtleff, *Records of the Governor and Company* 4(1):366.

37 "Abraham Arrington": See Paige, *History of Cambridge*, 540–41.

CHAPTER 4. TAVERN TALES

41 "Drinking with the Drummer": The court records include Hoadly, *Records of the Colony and Plantation of New Haven*, 379, 393–96, 429, 469; Hoadly, *Records of the Colony or Jurisdiction of New Haven*, 47–50, 54–57, 107–8. Other sources include Mayes, "An Independent Soul—Notes on Robert Bassett"; Orcutt, *A History of the Old Town of Stratford and the City of Bridgeport*, 1:255–60; Peachey, *The Tipler's Guide to Drink and Drinking*; Savage, *Genealogical Dictionary*, 1:136.

46 "Cider and Cakes for Highwaymen": The court records include Dow, *Records and Files of the Quarterly Courts of Essex County*, 6:54–56, 223, 229, 256–59, 295; 7:1, 2, 70–72, 77, 225, 401; 8:140.

47 "a tithingman": Tithingmen were originally appointed to maintain order during Sabbath services at Massachusetts meetinghouses—keeping adults awake and children quiet. By 1677 the duties were expanded throughout the week, and each tithingman was expected to monitor the morals of ten families in his neighborhood and, in the absence of the constable, apprehend drunkards and lawbreakers. Whitmore, *The Colonial Laws of Massachusetts*, 249–50.

"George Darling": Darling was one of the Scots captured by Oliver Cromwell during the English Civil War at the Battle of Dunbar and shipped to New England in 1650 on the *Unity* for servitude in the colonies. His name first appeared in New England court records as one of thirty-five Scottish workers listed in a 1653 inventory of property owned by the Hammersmith Ironworks in Lynn, Massachusetts. Other sources about George Darling and the Scots sold to the ironworks include Carlson, *The Scots at Hammersmith*, 13; Hartley, *Ironworks on the Saugus*; Rapaport, "Scottish Slavery in Seventeenth-Century New England," 44–52; Rapaport, "Scottish Slaves in Colonial New England."

CHAPTER 5. SLAVES AND SERVANTS

51 "The Irish Rebels": This story previously appeared in Diane Rapaport, "Tales from the Courthouse: The Case of the Irish Rebels," *New England Ancestors* 8 (Spring 2007): 55–56. Sources include Dow, *Records and Files of the Quarterly Courts of Essex County*, 2:197–98, 293–97, 310–11; 3:384, 462, 469; 4:86–87, 420; 5:124–25, 441; 6:192, 293, 359–60, 399; 7:23–24, 37, 67, 82, 238, 333, 336, 411; 8:5, 125, 179, 186; *New England Historical and Genealogical Register* 19 (1865): 55–56; *New England Historical and Genealogical Register* 23 (1869): 417–18; Welch, *Philip Welch of Ipswich, Massachusetts*, 3–17.

52 "an unsightly skin condition": The boys' exact ages at the time of their arrival cannot be determined with certainty, for the court records are inconsistent on that point. Perhaps the boys themselves did not know how old they were.

52 "official-looking bill of sale": The bill of sale erroneously referred to William Downing as William Dallton.

55 "Selling Silvanus Warro": This story previously appeared in Diane Rapaport, "Tales from the Courthouse: The Sale of Silvanus Warro," *New England Ancestors* 7 (Fall 2006): 53–54. The court records include Middlesex County (Massachusetts) Court Folio Collection, Folios 106, 112 and 44x; Middlesex County (Massachusetts) Court Minute Books, June 18, 1672, and October 19, 1682; Suffolk Files, Suffolk County (Massachusetts) Court Files, 1629–1797, no. 2104; Morison, *Records of the Suffolk County Court,* 1:113, 259. See also Gookin, *Daniel Gookin;* Morris, "'Sold to Maytence a Bastard': Sylvannus Warro's Story," 31–43; Nourse, *The Early Records of Lancaster, Massachusetts,* 92–93, 95; Thwing, *Inhabitants and Estates of the Town of Boston,* ref. code 30282.

"Gookin brought him to Massachusetts": Gookin also brought Silvanus Warro's brother, Daniel Warro, to Massachusetts. Both boys were young (apparently close in age), children of Gookin's slaves Jacob and Maria Warro, who stayed behind in Maryland to manage the plantation. See Morris, "'Sold to Maytence a Bastard.'"

56 "release Warro from slavery in 1675": At some point Gookin apparently emancipated Silvanus Warro's brother, Daniel. By 1676 Daniel was no longer a slave. See chapter 3.

57 "no intention of relinquishing him": Silvanus Warro managed a furtive trip back to Cambridge in January 1677, to visit Daniel and attend a Cambridge party. See chapter 3.

CHAPTER 6. NEIGHBOR VERSUS NEIGHBOR

59 "The Purloined Pigs": This story previously appeared in Diane Rapaport, "Tales from the Courthouse: The Case of the Purloined Pigs," *New England Ancestors* 5 (Winter 2004): 54–55, and was excerpted in Diane Rapaport, *New England Court Records: A Research Guide for Genealogists and Historians,* 389–90. The court records about this case, at the Judicial Archives/Massachusetts Archives, include Middlesex County (Massachusetts) Court Folio Collection 2, 59-2, *Row v. Bacon.* Other court records about Michael Bacon include Middlesex County (Massachusetts) Court Record Books (1648–63), 1:137–38, 166–67, 178; Middlesex County (Massachusetts) Court Folio Collection 16-5, 18 (Group IIIA and Group VG), 1670-55-2, 1672-61-3, 1676-71-2, 1676-72-2, and 55-II-1691. See also chapter 2. Read more about William Munro and the seventeenth-century Scottish war prisoners in Munro, *History and Genealogy of the Lexington, Mass. Munroes;* Rapaport, "Scots for Sale"; Rapaport, "Scottish Slavery in Seventeenth-Century New England"; Rapaport, "Scottish Slaves in Colonial New England."

"what we know about William Munro": According to local and family tradition, William was a Scottish survivor of the Battle of Worcester in 1651, captured by Oliver Cromwell and shipped to New England on the *John and Sarah* for servitude in the colonies. Although his full name does not appear on the *John and Sarah* transport list, a "Monrow" on the document whose first name was torn or obliterated is believed to have been William.

63 "Native Neighbors": This story previously appeared in Diane Rapaport, "Tales from the Courthouse: Coe's Case: Indians in Colonial Courts," *New England Ancestors* 6 (Spring 2005): 52–53. The court records are published in Smith, *Colonial Justice in Western Massachusetts,* 217, 223–24, 274, 323–25, 341–42; the original Pynchon court record manuscripts are archived at Harvard Law School: Pynchon, William, 1590–1662, Record of cases before the magistrate of Agawan, Springfield, Massachusetts, 1638–1702, HLS MS 4344, Harvard Law School Library.

66   "five fathom": See Jordan, "The Coins of Colonial and Early America."

"Springfield burned to the ground": See Bridenbaugh, *Pynchon Papers,* 146, 160–62.

"John Crowfoote": Despite the Native-sounding name, John Crowfoote apparently was not Indian. His father, Joseph Crowfoote (see Savage, *Genealogical Dictionary,* 1:480), was likely a Crawford from Scotland, one of the Scottish war prisoners exiled to New England in the mid-1600s. (*Crawford* spoken with a Scottish brogue could sound much like *Crowfoote* to a colonial clerk.)

67   "The Sudbury Standoff": Court records, at the Judicial Archives/Massachusetts Archives, include Middlesex County (Massachusetts) Court Record Books (1648–63), 1:83, 124, 135; Middlesex County (Massachusetts) Court Folio Collection, Folios 92X, 233, 237-2, 246. Related court and town records, some digitally reproduced, are available at www.sudbury.ma.us/archives: "The Sudbury Archives," record nos. 1350, 1353, 1386, 2579–80, 2583, 2732. Other sources include Emery, *The Puritan Village Evolves;* Fewkes, "The Book of Ross," 4:2701–20; Hudson, *The History of Sudbury, Massachusetts; New England Historical and Genealogical Register* 17 (1863): 254–58, 260, 312, 314; *New England Historical and Genealogical Register* 18 (1864): 141; Powell, *Puritan Village;* Powell, "The Sudbury Records, 1639–1695," 1:182, 188, 221–24.

69   "sold into servitude": Ross's name appears on a transport list of Scots shipped to New England on the *John and Sarah.* See Rapaport, "Scots for Sale."

"James rented a farm at first": Ross apparently rented the Sudbury farm owned by the former Harvard College president Henry Dunster. See Rodgers, *Middlesex County in the Colony of Massachusetts Bay, October 1649–December 1660,* 399, re: the June 1659 inventory of Henry Dunster's estate: "A farme at Sudbury rented to a Sckotch man, with a house, barne and 15 acres of meadow," valued at £160. See also chapter 7 for more about Henry Dunster.

70   "Paul Dudley": Dudley eventually became chief justice of the Massachusetts Superior Court of Judicature and the colony's attorney general. See Coquillette, *Law in Colonial Massachusetts,* xl, xliv, xxxiii n3, xxxiv, 9, 87–88, illus. 196, 197, 217, 283, 286, 330.

CHAPTER 7. SUNDAY MEETING

73   "The Naked Quaker": This story previously appeared in Diane Rapaport, "Tales from the Courthouse: The Case of the Naked Quaker," *New England Ancestors* 5 (Fall 2004): 49–50. Court records include Dow, *Records and Files of the Quarterly Courts of Essex County,* 1:81, 99, 235, 275, 378; 3:17, 60, 64, 68; 4:136–37, 243, 271, 5:232, 306, 308, 311; 7:406–7; Smith, *Colonial Justice in Western Massachusetts,* 252–53; Middlesex County (Massachusetts) Court Record Books (1648–63), 1:72–75, 134–35, 165, 286, 295; (1671–86), 12–14. Other sources include Pestana, *Quakers and Baptists in Colonial Massachusetts;* Shurtleff, *Records of the Governor and Company,* 3:415–16; 4(1):276, 321, 345–46, 349, 366–67, 383–90, 419, 433, 449–53; 4(2): 3–4, 20, 34, 43, 58–59, 88; Stouck, *The Wardells and Vosburghs,* 6, 7, 28–35, 52–71.

"to arrive at church on time": The meetinghouse in seventeenth-century New England was a multipurpose building—house of worship, town hall, and sometimes even an armory for weapons and gunpowder (which explains why the meetinghouse was unheated). To avoid confusion, this chapter generally uses the word *church* instead of *meetinghouse.*

78   "The Harvard Heretic": This story previously appeared in Diane Rapaport, "Tales from the Courthouse: The Case of the Harvard Heretic," *New England Ancestors* 7 (Holiday 2006): 59–61. Court records, at the Judicial Archives/Massachusetts

Archives, include Middlesex County (Massachusetts) Court Record Books (1649–63), 1:72–74, 132. For other court records, and further information about Dunster, see Chaplin, *Life of Henry Dunster;* Morison, *The Founding of Harvard College;* Shurtleff, *Records of the Governor and Company,* 3:352; 4(1):196–97, 312–13.

CHAPTER 8. FRONTIER JUSTICE

83 "Chesley and the 'Cheating Knave'": The court records are published in Hammond, *New Hampshire Court Records,* 20–21, 55–57, 83–84, 107–8, 111, 115, 126, 128, 200, 202, 211–12, 215, 235, 238, 246, 255, 265–66, 283, 295, 304, 373, 468, 474–77, 483–85, 490–97. Other sources include Candee, "Merchant and Millwright"; Forman, "Mill Sawing in Seventeenth-Century Massachusetts"; Hubbard, *History of the Indian Wars in New England,* 2:110; Noyes, et al., *Genealogical Dictionary of Maine and New Hampshire,* 52 (List 364), 139–40; Stackpole and Thompson, *History of the Town of Durham,* 1:3, 34, 65, 82, 102–6; 2:51–76.

88 "'Breaking the King's Peace'"; The court records are published in Libby, Moody, and Allen, *Province and Court Records of Maine,* 1:90, 104, 111, 119, 125–26, 134–35, 138–39, 147, 154, 164–65, 173, 175–77, 179–80, 199, 253, 263–64, 272, 288; 2:12, 14, 20, 22, 27, 31, 46, 52, 55–57, 82, 92–93, 214, 252, 263, 276, 284, 305, 335, 449, 456–60, 466, 468, 478, 494–95; 3:201, 211, 273; 4:20, 37, 50, 125. See also Noyes, et al., *Genealogical Dictionary of Maine and New Hampshire,* 65, 68, 195–96, 267–68, 292, 442, 475–76, 588, 679, 707–8, 760–61.

89 "Hugh Gullison": The Gullison surname sometimes appeared as Gunnison in the old court records. According to tradition, the family originally came from Sweden. See Noyes, et al., *Genealogical Dictionary of Maine and New Hampshire,* 292.

90 "for adultery with an Indian": See Shurtleff and Pulsifer, *Records of the Colony of New Plymouth,* 1:132, 5:107.

93 "'To Drive Away Melancholy'": The court records are published in Smith, *Colonial Justice in Western Massachusetts,* 225, 229–30, 243, 257–58, 263, 270. The original Pynchon court record manuscripts are archived at Harvard Law School: Pynchon, William, 1590–1662, Record of cases before the magistrate of Agawam, Springfield, Massachusetts, 1638–1702, HLS MS 4344, Harvard Law School Library. Other sources include Barbour, *Families of Early Hartford,* 292, 577; Parker, *History of the Second Church of Christ in Hartford,* 128; Roberts, *Historic Towns of the Connecticut River Valley;* Savage, *Genealogical Dictionary,* 2:404; 4:37.

"John Henryson": The name also appears in the various sources as Hannison, Hennyson, Henderson, etc.

"pregnant that winter": Genealogists differ about the birth date of John and Martha's first child, Elizabeth, the discrepancy possibly being due to confusion about calendar systems—Julian and Gregorian—both in use during the colonial period. Documentary sources, however, suggest that Martha was pregnant during the winter of 1661–62. In court records about the card playing, John Henryson said that he would do "anything when [his wife] was ill to make her merry." *Illness* was a common euphemism for pregnancy. Also, the Winthrop Medical Records (in the Winthrop Papers) contain notations about Elizabeth (with her age in various years) that are consistent with a January 1662 birth date and with the information in Warren, "Springfield Families."

94 "prosecuted—and punished—in court": In 1659 the Massachusetts General Court ordered: "Whereas . . . it is a custom too frequent in many places to expend time in unlawful games, as cards, dice, etc., it is therefore . . . ordered . . . that . . .

whosoever shall be found . . . playing either at cards or at dice . . . shall pay as a fine to the county the sum of five shillings for every such offense." Shurtleff, *Records of the Governor and Company,* 4(1):366–67.

94　"calling him a 'Scottish dog'": John Henryson undoubtedly was one of the former Scottish war prisoners from the Battle of Dunbar, exiled to New England in the mid-1600s and sold into servitude. Henryson probably met Martha in Hartford, perhaps as a servant in the Steele household.

97　"out-of-court falsehoods": Out-of-court lies, if "pernicious to the public weal," were against the law; see *The Laws and Liberties of Massachusetts,* s.v. "Lying, 35."

　"King Philip's War": See Bridenbaugh, *The Pynchon Papers.*

CHAPTER 9. OFFSHORE ANTICS

99　"The Captured *Fortune*": This story previously appeared in Diane Rapaport, "Tales from the Courthouse: The Case of the Captured *Fortune*," *New England Ancestors* 6 (Summer 2005): 51–52. Its source is Towle, *Records of the Vice-Admiralty Court,* 259–78.

103　"Smuttynose Sailors and Sinners": This story previously appeared in Diane Rapaport, "Tales from the Courthouse: Offshore Antics: The Case of the Smuttynose Sailor Who Became a Judge," *New England Ancestors* 5 (Summer 2004): 48–49, 55. The court records are published in Hammond, *New Hampshire Court Records,* 209–10, 312; Libby, Moody, and Allen, *Province and Court Records of Maine,* 1:104, 119, 289, 309; 2:167, 169, 171, 209, 217, 346; 3:3, 6, 61, 71, 118, 148, 159, 198, 280; 4:21, 131, 184–85, 203–4, 290–91, 312–13, 395; Cronin and Noble, *Records of the Court of Assistants,* 3:140; Morison, *Records of the Suffolk County Court,* 1:13. See also Noyes, et al., *Genealogical Dictionary of Maine and New Hampshire,* 247, 395–96, 518.

CHAPTER 10. LAWYERS AND JUDGES

109　"The Outspoken Advocate": This story previously appeared in Diane Rapaport, "Tales from the Courthouse: The Case of the Outspoken Advocate," *New England Ancestors* 6 (Fall 2005): 53–54. The court records are published in Cronin and Noble, *Records of the Court of Assistants,* 1:72, 164, 166, 219; 3:195–96; Morison, *Records of the Suffolk County Court,* 2:1125–30; Shurtleff, *Records of the Governor and Company,* 4(2):291–92, 301, 387; 5:82, 117, 359. Other sources include Rowlandson, *Narrative of the Captivity,* 47–50, 53–55; Nourse, "The Ancestry of the Hoar Family in America," 186–98; Schultz and Tougias, *King Philip's War,* 185–93; Thomas, *Diary of Samuel Sewall,* 1:269.

　"a surprise attack on Lancaster, Massachusetts": Although Hoar lived in Concord, Massachusetts, he had a personal interest in the fate of Lancaster. His eldest daughter, Elizabeth, married Jonathan Prescott, son of a Lancaster founder, just two months before the attack. The Prescotts survived, but fifty-five Lancaster residents and defenders did not, and the town was reduced to ashes.

110　"John Hoar's early life": Born in England about 1622 and apprenticed in the brewing trade, Hoar migrated to New England with his siblings and widowed mother. He lived in Scituate from the 1640s, then bought land in Concord, Massachusetts, by 1659.

113　"Captain Barefoot Goes to Court": This story previously appeared in Diane Rapaport, "Tales from the Courthouse: Captain Barefoot Goes to Court," *New England Ancestors* 6 (Winter 2005): 48–49. Court records involving Walter Barefoot include these published sources: Dow, *Records and Files of the Quarterly Courts of Essex County,* 3:1, 48, 58,

76, 90, 106, 182, 194–97, 239, 319, 450; 4:22, 61–66, 112, 129, 133, 184, 236, 303–4; 5:98, 101, 148, 150, 164, 301, 406; 6:22, 24, 142, 211, 263, 429; 7:191; Hammond, *New Hampshire Court Records,* 171–72, 179–80, 198, 206–10, 217, 225, 227, 233–36, 245, 256–57, 262, 267–68, 277–80, 291–92, 307, 314, 316, 324, 326–27, 350, 373, 391, 396, 536; Libby, Moody, and Allen, *Province and Court Records of Maine,* 1:280; 2:101, 114, 131, 211, 234–35, 256, 277–78, 298, 312, 333, 340, 372, 379, 441–45; 3:17; Morison, *Records of the Suffolk County Court,* 1:4, 13–16, 64, 86–87, 102, 144, 299–300; Cronin and Noble, *Records of the Court of Assistants,* 1:67, 3:194, 211–12, 239–40; Shurtleff, *Records of the Governor and Company,* 4(2):426, 454–55, 526, 529, 557; 5:149. See also Noyes, et al., *Genealogical Dictionary of Maine and New Hampshire,* 76; Savage, *Genealogical Dictionary,* 1:114–15.

115   "powerful family connections": Barefoot also had his own family connection with Andrew Wiggin. Barefoot's sister Sarah was married to Andrew's brother, Thomas Wiggin. See Noyes, et al., *Genealogical Dictionary of Maine and New Hampshire,* 751–53.

117   "'A True New England Man'": The court records include Middlesex County (Massachusetts) Court Record Books (1648–63), 1:294–96, 300; Rodgers, *Middlesex County in the Colony of the Massachusetts Bay, March 1660/61–December 1670,* 120, 575. Other sources, many of which include portions of court records, are Cogley, *John Eliot's Mission to the Indians;* May, *Danforth Genealogy;* Paige, *History of Cambridge,* 346–47, 394–95, 530; Roach, *The Salem Witch Trials;* Thomas, *Diary of Samuel Sewall,* 1:416–17; Thompson, *Cambridge Cameos;* Thompson, "The Transit of Civilization," 37–44.

118   "who lived in another town": See *Proceedings of the Massachusetts Historical Society* 13:305-06.

120   "a century before the American Revolution": See Moody and Simmons, *The Glorious Revolution in Massachusetts.*

122   "'Salem End'": See Herring, *Framingham,* and Keener, "Bewitched by History."

ILLUSTRATION SOURCES

Illustrations are listed by page number.

3 From Edward R. Lambert, *History of the Colony of New Haven* (New Haven: Hitchcock and Stafford, 1838).

10 Middlesex County (Massachusetts) Court Folio Collection, Folio 25, Group 1B, *Winifred and Mary Holman v. John Gibson and Family,* March 28, 1659/60. Courtesy of Judicial Archives/ Massachusetts Archives. (Special thanks to Elizabeth Bouvier, Head of Archives for the Supreme Judicial Court of Massachusetts, and to Jennifer Fauxsmith, Reference Archivist for the Massachusetts Archives.)

13 "Whipping at the Cart's Tayle." Illustration by Frank Hazenplug, from Alice Morse Earle, *Curious Punishments of Bygone Days* (Chicago: H. S. Stone, 1896).

23 "The Stocks." Illustration by Frank Hazenplug, from Alice Morse Earle, *Curious Punishments of Bygone Days* (Chicago: H. S. Stone, 1896).

26 Middlesex County (Massachusetts) Court Folio Collection, 1670, 55-2, *John Ball v. Michael Bacon,* June 21, 1671. Courtesy of Judicial Archives/Massachusetts Archives.

30 Illustration by Mary Weston Dodge, from Harriet Silvester Tapley, *Chronicles of Danvers (Old Salem Village), 1632–1923* (Danvers, Mass.: Danvers Historical Society, 1923), 12. Courtesy of Danvers Historical Society.

39 From Harvard College Disorders Papers, UAI 15.350VT. Courtesy of the Harvard University Archives, call no. UAI 15.350 vt, p. 14. (Special thanks to Megan Sniffin-Marinoff, University Archivist, and Kyle DeCicco-Carey, Reference Assistant.)

42 Drum and tankard © 2007 Cary Rapaport; all rights reserved. Courtesy of Cary Rapaport.

48 Two seventeenth-century horsemen. From the frontispiece of *The English Rogue Containing a brief Discovery of the most Eminent Cheats, Robberies, and other Extravagantcies [sic], by him Committed* (London: Printed for J. Blare, at the Looking-Glass, on London-Bridge, 1688). Courtesy of Gillian Spraggs, author of *Outlaws and Highwaymen: The Cult of the Robber in England from the Middle Ages to the Nineteenth Century* (London: Pimlico, 2001); illustration from her Web site, www.outlawsandhighwaymen.com.

53 From Augustine Caldwell, ed., *Ipswich Antiquarian Papers* (Ipswich, Mass., 1883).

58 From Frederick William Gookin, *Daniel Gookin, 1612–1687: Assistant and Major General of the Massachusetts Bay Colony* (Chicago: Privately printed, 1912).

63 Middlesex County (Massachusetts) Court Folio Collection 2, 59-2, December 2, 1671. Courtesy of Judicial Archives/Massachusetts Archives. (Special thanks to Elizabeth Bouvier, Head of Archives for the Supreme Judicial Court of Massachusetts, and to Jennifer Fauxsmith, Reference Archivist for the Massachusetts Archives.)

65 Diary of William Pynchon, May 4, 1648 (p. 25), *Coe v. Francis Ball.* From William Pynchon, 1590–1662, Record of Cases before the Magistrate of Agawan, Springfield, Mass., 1638–1702, HLS MS 4344, Hollis no. 002230861. Courtesy of Special Collections Department, Harvard Law School Library. (Special thanks to David Warrington, Head of Special Collections, and to Lesley Schoenfeld, Access Services Coordinator.)

68   First Parish, Unitarian Universalist Church, Wayland, Massachusetts, 2007. Photograph by the author.

74   "Public Penance." Illustration by Frank Hazenplug, from Alice Morse Earle, *Curious Punishments of Bygone Days* (Chicago: H. S. Stone, 1896).

79   From Rev. Jeremiah Chaplin, *Life of Henry Dunster* (Boston: James R. Osgood, 1872).

85   "Felling." © 1977 S. F. Manning; all rights reserved. Courtesy of Samuel F. Manning, from his book, *New England Masts and the King's Broad Arrow* (1979; rept., Gardiner, Maine: Tilbury House, 2000); originally commissioned for the 1977 TV documentary *Home to the Sea,* a production of the Maine Public Broadcasting Network.

87   From Everett S. Stackpole and Lucien Thompson, *History of the Town of Durham, New Hampshire (Oyster River Plantation) with Genealogical Notes,* 2 vols. (Concord, N.H.: Rumford Press, 1913).

91   From Everett S. Stackpole, *Old Kittery and Her Families* (Lewiston, Maine: Press of Lewiston Journal Co., 1903).

95   Diary of John Pynchon, March 20, 1661/62 (p. 97). From William Pynchon, 1590–1662, Record of Cases before the Magistrate of Agawan, Springfield, Mass., 1638–1702, HLS MS 4344, Hollis no. 002230861. Courtesy of Special Collections Department, Harvard Law School Library. (Special thanks to David Warrington, Head of Special Collections, and to Lesley Schoenfeld, Access Services Coordinator.)

100   "Departure." © 1977 S. F. Manning; all rights reserved. Courtesy of Samuel F. Manning, from his book, *New England Masts and the King's Broad Arrow* (1979; rept., Gardiner, Maine: Tilbury House, 2000); originally commissioned for the 1977 TV documentary *Home to the Sea,* a production of the Maine Public Broadcasting Network.

104   From John Scribner Jenness, *The Isles of Shoals: An Historical Sketch* (Cambridge, Mass.: Riverside Press, 1873).

107   From John Scribner Jenness, *The Isles of Shoals: An Historical Sketch* (Cambridge, Mass.: Riverside Press, 1873).

111   Photograph of Redemption Rock (Route 140, Princeton, Massachusetts), a protected property of the Trustees of Reservations, www.thetrustees.org. Courtesy of the Trustees of Reservations.

112   From Daniel Strock Jr., *Pictorial History of King Philip's War* (Hartford: Case, Tiffany, 1852).

114   From William Hubbard, *The History of the Indian Wars in New England: From the First Settlement to the Termination of the War with King Philip, in 1677,* 2 vols. (1677; revised and supplemented by Samuel G. Drake, 1864).

117   From Middlesex County (Massachusetts) Court Folio Collection, 1678, 80-3, *Daniel Wiman v. Michael Bacon,* July 29, 1678. Courtesy of Judicial Archives/Massachusetts Archives. (Special thanks to Elizabeth Bouvier, Head of Archives for the Supreme Judicial Court of Massachusetts, and to Jennifer Fauxsmith, Reference Archivist for the Massachusetts Archives.)

121   From Frederick William Gookin, *Daniel Gookin, 1612–1687: Assistant and Major General of the Massachusetts Bay Colony* (Chicago: Privately printed, 1912).

BIBLIOGRAPHY

Baldwin, Thomas W. *Michael Bacon and His Descendants.* Cambridge, Mass., 1915.

Barbour, Lucius Barnes. *Families of Early Hartford, Connecticut.* Baltimore: Genealogical Publishing Co., 1982.

Bodge, George M. "Soldiers in King Philip's War." *New England Historical and Genealogical Register* 37 (1883).

Bond, Henry. *Family Memorials:Genealogies of the Families and Descendants of the Early Settlers of Watertown, Massachusetts.* 2 vols. Boston: Little, Brown and Company, 1855.

Bridenbaugh, Carl, ed. *The Pynchon Papers, vol. 1, Letters of John Pynchon, 1654–1700.* Boston: Colonial Society of Massachusetts, 1982.

Candee, Richard M. "Merchant and Millwright: The Water Powered Sawmills of the Piscataqua." *Old-Time New England* 60, no. 4 (1970): 131–49.

Carlson, Stephen P. *The Scots at Hammersmith.* Saugus, Mass.: Eastern National Park and Monument Association, 1976.

Chaplin, Rev. Jeremiah. *Life of Henry Dunster.* Boston: James R. Osgood, 1872.

Cogley, Richard W. *John Eliot's Mission to the Indians before King Philip's War.* Cambridge: Harvard University Press, 1999.

Coquillette, Daniel R., ed. *Law in Colonial Massachusetts, 1630–1800.* Boston: Colonial Society of Massachusetts, 1984.

Cronin, John F., and John Noble, eds. *Records of the Court of Assistants of the Colony of the Massachusetts Bay, 1630–1692.* 3 vols. Boston: County of Suffolk, 1901–28.

Cutter, William Richard. *Genealogical and Personal Memoirs Relating to the Families of the State of Massachusetts.* 4 vols. New York: Lewis Historical Publishing Co., 1910.

Dexter, Franklin Bowditch, ed. *Ancient Town Records, New Haven Town Records 1649–1684.* 2 vols. New Haven: New Haven Colony Historical Society, 1917, 1919.

Dow, George Francis, ed. *The Probate Records of Essex County, Massachusetts.* 3 vols. Salem: Essex Institute, 1916–20.

————. *Records and Files of the Quarterly Courts of Essex County, Massachusetts.* 9 vols. Salem: Essex Institute, 1911–75.

Emery, Helen Fitch. *The Puritan Village Evolves: A History of Wayland, Massachusetts.* Canaan, N.H.: Phoenix Publishing, for the Wayland Historical Commission, 1981.

Essex County Quarterly Court File Papers, WPA Transcripts, 6/26/1–3; 10/34/1–10/37/1, 10/37/3–6 (microfilm, available at the Judicial Archives/Massachusetts Archives).

Fewkes, Ernest E. "The Book of Ross" (1927). Typescript, R. Stanton Avery Special Collections, New England Historic Genealogical Society, Boston.

Forman, Benno M. "Mill Sawing in Seventeenth-Century Massachusetts." *Old-Time New England* 60, no. 4 (1970): 110–30.

Godman, Percy S. *Some Account of the Family of Godman.* London, 1897.

Gookin, Frederick William. *Daniel Gookin, 1612–1687: Assistant and Major General of the Massachusetts Bay Colony.* Chicago: Privately printed, 1912.

Hall, David D., ed. *Witch-Hunting in Seventeenth-Century New England: A Documentary History, 1638–1692.* Boston: Northeastern University Press, 1991.

Hammond, Otis G., ed. *New Hampshire Court Records 1640–1692, Court Papers 1652–1668, State Papers Series, Vol. 40.* Concord: State of New Hampshire, 1943.

Hartley, E. N. *Ironworks on the Saugus.* Norman: University of Oklahoma Press, 1957.

Herring, Stephen. *Framingham: An American Town.* Framingham, Mass.: Framingham Historical Society, 2000.

Hoadly, Charles J., ed. *Records of the Colony and Plantation of New Haven, from 1638 to 1649.* Hartford: Case, Tiffany, 1857; full text also available at www.books.google.com.

————. *Records of the Colony or Jurisdiction of New Haven, from May, 1653, to the Union: Together with the New Haven Code of 1656.* Hartford: Case, Lockwood, 1858; full text also available at www.books.google.com.

Hubbard, William. *The History of the Indian Wars in New England: From the First Settlement to the Termination of the War with King Philip, in 1677.* 2 vols. 1677; revised and supplemented by Samuel G. Drake, 1864; reprint, Bowie, Md.: Heritage Books, 1990.

Hudson, Alfred S. *The History of Sudbury, Massachusetts, 1638–1889.* 1889; reprint, Sudbury, Mass.: Sudbury Press, 1968.

Jordan, Louis. "The Coins of Colonial and Early America." Notre Dame, Ind.: University of Notre Dame, Department of Special Collections. www.coins.nd.edu/ColCoin/ColCoinIntros/NNWampum.html.

Kamensky, Jane. *Governing the Tongue: The Politics of Speech in Early New England.* New York: Oxford University Press, 1997.

Keener, Jessica Brilliant. "Bewitched by History." *Boston Globe Magazine,* December 17, 2000.

The Laws and Liberties of Massachusetts: Reprinted from the Unique Copy of the 1648 Edition in the Henry E. Huntington Library. San Marino, Calif.: Huntington Library, 1998.

Lepore, Jill. *The Name of War: King Philip's War and the Origins of American Identity.* New York: Alfred A. Knopf, 1998.

Libby, Charles Thornton, Robert E. Moody, and Neal W. Allen Jr., eds. *Province and Court Records of Maine.* 6 vols. Portland: Maine Historical Society, 1928–75.

Mather, Cotton. *Magnalia Christi Americana.* 2 vols. 1702; reprint, Hartford, Conn.: Silas Andrus, 1820.

May, John Joseph, comp. *Danforth Genealogy: Nicholas Danforth, of Framlingham, England, and Cambridge, N.E. (1589–1638). . . .* Boston: Charles H. Pope, 1902.

Mayes, D. "An Independent Soul—Notes on Robert Bassett." www.horsethief.info/bassett/bassettb3.htm.

Middlesex County (Massachusetts) Court Folio Collection. Folios 25, 44x, 92x, 106, 112, 233, 237, and 246. Judicial Archives/Massachusetts Archives.

Middlesex County (Massachusetts) Court Record Books (1649–63), Pulsifer Transcript. Judicial Archives/Massachusetts Archives.

Middlesex County (Massachusetts) Court Record Books (1671–86), Pulsifer Transcript. Judicial Archives/Massachusetts Archives.

Moody, Robert E., and Richard C. Simmons, eds. *The Glorious Revolution in Massachusetts: Selected Documents, 1689–1692.* Boston: Colonial Society of Massachusetts, 1988.

Morison, Samuel Eliot. *The Founding of Harvard College.* 1935; reprint, Cambridge: Harvard University Press, 1995.

————. *Harvard College in the Seventeenth Century.* 2 vols. Cambridge: Harvard University Press, 1936.

————, ed., *Records of the Suffolk County Court, 1671–1680,* 2 vols. Publications of the Colonial Society of Massachusetts, 1933.

Morris, M. Michelle Jarrett. "'Sold to Maytence a Bastard': Sylvannus Warro's Story." In Peter Benes, ed., *Slavery/Antislavery in New England* (Dublin Seminar for New England Folklife, Annual Proceedings 2003). Boston: Boston University, 2005.

Munro, R. S. *History and Genealogy of the Lexington, Mass.* Munroes. 2d ed. Florence, Mass.: By the author, 1986.

Music in Colonial Massachusetts, 1630-1820, A Conference Held by the Colonial Society of Massachusetts May 17 and 18, 1973. 2 vols. Boston: Colonial Society of Massachusetts, 1980–85.

New England Historical and Genealogical Register 1 (1847).

New England Historical and Genealogical Register 17 (1863).

New England Historical and Genealogical Register 18 (1864).

New England Historical and Genealogical Register 19 (1865).

New England Historical and Genealogical Register 23 (1869).

Norton, Mary Beth. *Founding Mothers and Fathers.* New York: Alfred A. Knopf, 1996.

Nourse, Henry S. "The Ancestry of the Hoar Family in America." *New England Historical and Genealogical Register* 53 (1889): 186–98.

————. *The Early Records of Lancaster, Massachusetts, 1643–1725.* Lancaster, Mass.: W. J. Coulter, 1884.

Noyes, Sybil, et al. *Genealogical Dictionary of Maine and New Hampshire.* Portland, Me.: Southworth-Anthoensen Press, 1928–39.

Orcutt, Samuel. *A History of the Old Town of Stratford and the City of Bridgeport, Connecticut.* 2 vols. New Haven, Conn.: Tuttle, Morehouse and Taylor, 1886.

Paige, Lucius R. *History of Cambridge, Massachusetts, 1630–1877.* With a Genealogical Register. 1877, reprint, Bowie, Md.: Heritage Books, 1986.

Parker, Edwin Pond. *History of the Second Church of Christ in Hartford.* Hartford: Belknap and Warfield, 1892.

Peachey, Stuart. *The Tipler's Guide to Drink and Drinking in the Early 17th Century.* Bristol, U.K.: Stuart Press, 1992.

Peirce, Frederick Clifton. *Peirce Genealogy, Being the Record of the Posterity of John Pers, an Early Inhabitant of Watertown, in New England.* Worcester, Mass.: Press of Chas. Hamilton, 1880.

Pestana, Carla Gardina. *Quakers and Baptists in Colonial Massachusetts.* New York: Cambridge University Press, 1991.

Powell, Sumner Chilton. *Puritan Village: The Formation of a New England Town.* Middletown, Conn.: Wesleyan University Press, 1963.

————, ed. "The Sudbury Records, 1639–1695." Typescript at Sudbury Public Library, Sudbury, Mass.

Pramberg, Noreen C. "He Led Two Lives: Jonathan Dunham, alias Singletary." *Essex Genealogist* 21 (2001): 144–47.

Proceedings of the Massachusetts Historical Society 13 (1873–75).

Rapaport, Diane. *New England Court Records: A Research Guide for Genealogists and Historians.* Burlington, Mass.: Quill Pen Press, 2006.

———. "Scots for Sale: The Fate of the Scottish Prisoners in Seventeenth-Century Massachusetts." *New England Ancestors* 4 (Winter 2003): 30–32; also published in an expanded version at www.NewEnglandAncestors.org.

———. "Scots for Sale, Part II: Scottish Prisoners in Seventeenth-Century Maine and New Hampshire." *New England Ancestors* 5 (Holiday 2004):26–28.

———. "Scottish Slavery in Seventeenth-Century New England." *History Scotland* 5 (January–February 2005): 44–52.

———. "Scottish Slaves in Colonial New England." *Highlander* 42 (September–October and November–December 2004).

Roach, Marilynne K. *The Salem Witch Trials: A Day-by-Day Chronicle of a Community under Siege.* New York: Cooper Square Press, 2002.

Roberts, George S. *Historic Towns of the Connecticut River Valley.* Schenectady, N.Y.: Robson and Adee, 1906.

Rodgers, Robert H. *Middlesex County in the Colony of the Massachusetts Bay in New England: Records of Probate and Administration, October 1649–December 1660.* Boston: New England Historic Genealogical Society, 1999.

———. *Middlesex County in the Colony of the Massachusetts Bay in New England: Records of Probate and Administration, March 1660/61–December 1670.* Boston: New England Historic Genealogical Society, 2001.

Rowlandson, Mary. *The Narrative of the Captivity and Restoration of Mrs. Mary Rowlandson.* 1682; reprint, Lancaster, Mass.: By the Town, 1975.

Savage, James, ed. *A Genealogical Dictionary of the First Settlers of New England.* Boston: Little, Brown and Company, 1860–62.

Schultz, Eric B., and Michael J. Tougias. *King Philip's War: The History and Legacy of America's Forgotten Conflict.* Woodstock, Vt.: Countryman Press, 1999.

Shurtleff, Nathaniel B., ed. *Records of the Colony of New Plymouth in New England, Court Orders: Vol. VI, 1678–1691.* 1856; reprint, Bowie, Md.: Heritage Books, 1998.

———. *Records of the Governor and Company of the Massachusetts Bay in New England.* 5 vols. in 6. Boston: W. White, 1853–54.

Shurtleff, Nathaniel B., and David Pulsifer, eds. *Records of the Colony of New Plymouth in New England,* 12 vols. Boston: White, 1855–61.

Sibley, John Langdon. *Biographical Sketches of Graduates of Harvard University, in Cambridge, Massachusetts.* Boston: Massachusetts Historical Society, 1873– .

Smith, John Langdon, ed. *Colonial Justice in Western Massachusetts (1639–1702): The Pynchon Court Record, an Original Judges' Diary of the Administration of Justice in the Springfield Courts in the Massachusetts Bay Colony.* Cambridge: Harvard University Press, 1961.

Stackpole, Everett S., and Lucien Thompson. *History of the Town of Durham, New Hampshire (Oyster River Plantation) with Genealogical Notes.* 2 vols. Concord, N.H.: Rumford Press, 1913.

Stouck, David. *The Wardells and Vosburghs: Records of a Loyalist Family.* Jordan, Ontario: Jordan Historical Museum, 1986.

Suffolk County (Massachusetts) Court Files, 1629–1797. Judicial Archives/Massachusetts Archives.

Thomas, M. Halsey, ed. *The Diary of Samuel Sewall, 1674–1729*. 2 vols. New York: Farrar, Straus and Giroux, 1973.

Thompson, Roger. *Cambridge Cameos: Stories of Life in Seventeenth-Century New England*. Boston: New England Historic Genealogical Society, 2005.

———. "The Transit of Civilization: The Case of Thomas Danforth." In Winfried Herget and Karl Ortseifen, eds., *The Transit of Civilization from Europe to America: Essays in Honor of Hans Galinsky*. Tübingen, Germany: Gunter Narr Verlag, 1986.

Thwing, Annie Haven. *Inhabitants and Estates of the Town of Boston 1630–1800 and The Crooked and Narrow Streets of Boston 1630–1822*. Boston: New England Historic Genealogical Society, 2001, CD-ROM.

Towle, Dorothy S., ed. *Records of the Vice-Admiralty Court of Rhode Island: 1716–1752*. 1936; reprint, Millwood, N.Y.: Kraus Reprint Co., 1975.

Waggener, Rick. "Notes for Jonathan Dunham alias Singletary," http://freepages.genealogy.rootsweb.com/~grannyapple/DUNHAM/SingletaryDunham History.html.

Walroth, Joanne Ruth. "Beyond Legal Remedy: Divorce in Seventeenth-Century Woodbridge, New Jersey." *Proceedings of the New Jersey Historical Society* 108 (1987): 1–18.

Warren, Thomas B. "Springfield Families." In *Families of the Pioneer Valley*. W. Springfield, Mass: Regional Publications, 2000, CD-ROM.

Watertown Records. Multiple vols. Watertown, Mass.: Watertown Historical Society, 1894– .

Welch, Alexander McMillan. *Philip Welch of Ipswich, Massachusetts, 1654, and His Descendants*. Richmond, Va.: William Byrd Press, 1947.

Whitmore, William H., ed. *The Colonial Laws of Massachusetts*. Reprinted from the Edition of 1672, with the Supplements through 1686. Boston: Rockwell and Churchill, 1887.

Winthrop Papers: Bound Manuscripts. Medical Records, 1657–69. Winthrop Papers Microfilm, reel 38. Massachusetts Historical Society.

Wyman, Thomas Bellows. "Abstract of Middlesex Court Files," MSS 596. Handwritten transcription in 2 vols., 1649–64 and 1664–75. R. Stanton Avery Special Collections, New England Historic Genealogical Society, Boston (also available in a searchable database at www.NewEnglandAncestors.org).

INDEX

DIANE RAPAPORT, a former trial lawyer, has made a new career as an author and speaker, bringing history to life with true stories from early New England court records. Her articles for *New England Ancestors,* some of which appear in *The Naked Quaker,* have earned three "Excellence in Writing" awards from the International Society of Family History Writers and Editors. Her first book, *New England Court Records: A Research Guide for Genealogists and Historians,* received three 2007 Benjamin Franklin awards from PMA, the Independent Book Publishers Association. She lives in Lexington, Massachusetts.